NORTH YORKSHIRE
Strange but True

ROBERT WOODHOUSE

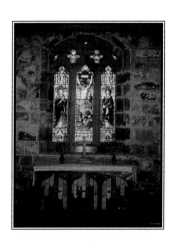

Sutton Publishing Limited
Phoenix Mill · Thrupp · Stroud
Gloucestershire · GL5 2BU

First published 2003

Copyright © Robert Woodhouse, 2003

Title page photograph: The chancel of St Mary's
Church, Over Silton.

**British Library Cataloguing in
Publication Data**
A catalogue record for this book is available
from the British Library.

ISBN 0-7509-3155-8

Typeset in 11/13 Photina.
Typesetting and origination by
Sutton Publishing Limited.
Printed and bound in England by
J.H. Haynes & Co. Ltd, Sparkford.

Ripon's Spa Hydro.

Contents

The obelisk in the graveyard at St Mary's Church, Bolton-on-Swale, marking the final resting place of Henry Jenkins who is alleged to have lived to the age of one hundred and sixty-nine.

Introduction

Most surveys of an area's history focus on the achievements of notable individuals, stirring battles and grand occasions. More often than not unusual characters, unlikely events and aspects of folklore tend to be overlooked. This collection of material from North Yorkshire's varied past takes a closer look at the lives of several eccentric personalities, curious structures that have become known as follies, natural landscape features (with barely credible outlines) and manmade puzzles fashioned in stone and turf. This amazing collection of oddities includes a number of over-ambitious schemes that never actually operated, as well as the elusive elements of truth and falsehood surrounding aspects of folklore involving monsters, giants, superstitions and the devil himself. Strange as they may seem, and however highly improbable they appear, the basis of truth is out there somewhere.

Shandy Hall, Coxwold, home of Laurence Sterne.

St Gregory's Church, Bedale.

1 Eccentric Individuals

After the border warfare and religious upheavals of earlier centuries peaceful times returned to northern England during the eighteenth century. Large landed estates were developed and this gave members of the privileged class, usually men but occasionally women, opportunities to indulge themselves. Financially secure and with time on their hands they could pursue interests in rural sports, entertaining and gambling, and this inevitably led to displays of more outlandish behaviour – as seen with John Hall Stevenson and George Osbaldeston. Others displayed a range of endearing idiosyncrasies, as in the case of Margaret Wharton, although these were seen as eccentric by her contemporaries, and there were always unscrupulous characters (such as John Wrightson) who were prepared to capitalise on the ignorance and gullibility of humble folk whose lives were governed by a fear of malevolent supernatural forces.

JOHN HALL STEVENSON

Born in 1718, John Hall began studies for a degree at Jesus College, Cambridge, on 16 June 1735 but left three years later without a degree to embark on the Grand Tour of Europe. Christened John Hall, he added his wife's surname (Stevenson) after inheriting the Skelton Castle estates on his mother's death. With time and money to spare, Stevenson repeatedly declared that his sole aim in life was to amuse himself. He did not share the interest of many of his contemporaries in field sports and divided his time between literature and entertaining guests.

Stevenson's library at Skelton included a large number of witty or humorous books and his group of friends shared his light-hearted outlook on life. Robert Lascelles (a clergyman), Zachary Moore, Andrew Irvine of Kirkleatham (a schoolmaster), Colonel Lee and an

Skelton Castle, family home of Margaret Wharton and John Hall Stevenson.

architect named Pringle joined Hall Stevenson to form a 'club of demoniacs' who met several times a year at Skelton to indulge in a round of drinking and jesting.

During the periods between such orgies Stevenson wrote a number of pamphlets, which gained a very mixed reception. A *Lyric Epistle*, published in 1760, was addressed to his friend from university days, Laurence Sterne, following publication of *Tristram Shandy*, but Stevenson's work was described by Thomas Gray as 'absolute nonsense'.

Several editions of *Crazy Tales* were issued. The book included descriptions of the wild parties at Skelton Castle. Some contemporaries such as Horace Walpole saw a 'vast deal of original humour and wit' in Stevenson's work, but other writers and critics were usually contemptuous in their comments, which appeared in the *Critical Review*. Scathing criticism only seems to have fired his appetite for

Skelton Castle in more modern times, with the local hunt gathering on the lawns to the south of the main buildings.

producing robust counter-attacks in verse. In 1760 he published a number of pamphlets including *A Nosegay and a Smile for the Reviewers* which contained retorts to his critics. Meetings with John Wilkes led to an interest in politics and a number of pamphlets, in which he attacked both Whigs and Tories, appeared during the 1760s.

Hall Stevenson's friendship with Sterne continued up to the latter's death in 1769. He features in *Tristram Shandy* and *Sentimental Journey* under the name Eugenius and in these works he is portrayed as a prudent counsellor. This seems to be linked with his patronage of the author. For Stevenson's part he seems to have imitated Sterne in many respects. He referred to him as 'cousin Shandy', often signed himself 'Anthony Shandy' and tried to imitate Sterne's style in *A Sentimental Dialogue between two souls in the palpable Body of an English Lady of*

Quantity and an Irish Gentleman, published in 1768. Sterne often stayed at Skelton Castle where he made use of the library, and during the summer of 1767 he and Stevenson raced each other in chariots along the nearby seashore.

In his later years John Hall Stevenson became an extreme hypochondriac and his misery was made worse by financial difficulties and an unhappy marriage. Writing to his grandson on 17 February 1785 he outlined his financial problems and blamed an early marriage for missing out on the many pleasures in life that had not come his way. He died at Skelton Castle in March 1785.

SQUIRE GEORGE OSBALDESTON

Down the years gambling debts have brought the downfall of many a man, but few can have enjoyed such an extravagant lifestyle as Squire George Osbaldeston of Ebberston. The family home was at Hutton Buscel, near Scarborough, but George was born in Wimpole Street, London, in 1787, where his mother had travelled in search of expert medical care. He inherited the Hutton Buscel estate at an early age, only to see the family mansion destroyed by fire in 1810, and some four years later George Osbaldeston bought Ebberston Hall on the north side of the Scarborough–Pickering road.

Built in 1718 by William Thompson, MP for Scarborough, this delightful Palladian style villa has been variously described as a folly, a lodge, a shooting box and, by its architect, Colen Campbell, as a 'Rustick Edifice'. It may well have been the water gardens that attracted George Osbaldeston to Ebberston. Soon after acquiring the estate he demolished two wings of the hall and used the stone to build stables, which provided the 1836 Derby winner, Ebberston. He probably intended to rebuild and extend Ebberston Hall on the grand scale in keeping with his self-styled title of 'Squire of all England' but mounting debts ruled out ambitious future plans.

George Osbaldeston's all-round sporting prowess showed through during his youth while he was still a student at Eton and Oxford, and his achievements soon assumed legendary proportions. Outstanding talent as a boxer, rower, tennis player and cricketer was matched by supreme skill with duelling pistols and guns on the grouse moors. Liberal amounts of

The south front of Ebberston Hall, home of Squire George Osbaldeston.

arrogance and stamina resulted in further amazing performances which included a billiards match spanning fifty hours of unbroken play, victories in rowing contests on the Thames during his forties and a narrow defeat on his own horse in a race at Goodwood when he was sixty-eight years of age. Some reports of Squire Osbaldeston's escapades stretch the bounds of credulity. During a dinner party it seems he was totally outraged by suggestions that his lady companion's posy was rather less impressive than others on display, and he promptly rode some 50 miles to bring back a garland that overshadowed all the rest.

As his gambling debts continued to mount, George Osbaldeston simply raised the stakes. On one occasion he gambled that he could cover the 200 miles around Newmarket Heath in ten hours and promptly completed the circuit in less than nine hours, which included a meal break. Spiralling debts led to speculative business ventures such as prospecting for coal deposits and opening lime kilns –

The entrance to Ebberston Hall.

but in the end there was no way out of these enormous financial problems and Squire Osbaldeston began to sell off parts of the estate. During 1848 he sold Ebberston Hall, and was only saved from complete ruination by the firm guidance of Mrs Williams, a level-headed widow who took a close interest in his welfare and restricted his wagers to just £1 each night.

George Osbaldeston died in 1866 but Ebberston Hall, setting for many of his outrageous exploits, holds an intriguing reminder of his lavish lifestyle. Along the parapet are engraved the outlines of hands and feet, which are said to be those of his many lady friends who were entertained at this tiny gem of a mansion. His faults may have been many but the world would certainly have been a duller place without Squire George Osbaldeston.

MARGARET WHARTON OF SKELTON

Eccentricity is after all a matter of opinion, isn't it? One person's perception of eccentric behaviour may well be seen by others as a pretty normal way of going on but Margaret Wharton of Skelton in Cleveland seems to have been widely regarded by her contemporaries as an extremely wealthy and highly eccentric old lady.

Born in 1688, she remained unmarried and accumulated a fortune, through thrifty management of the estate and her penny-pinching personal lifestyle, in excess of £200,000, half of which she is said to have given to her nephew, John Hall Stevenson. Much of the rest of her wealth was given away secretly in acts of charity and she then chose to live frugally.

Margaret Wharton spent some time in York and from there she travelled to Scarborough for summer holidays. It was during these coastal breaks that she is said to have often sent out for a pennyworth of strawberries and a pennyworth of cream, and this led to her nickname of 'Peg Pennyworth'. Her bouts of curious behaviour were dramatised by the playwright Samuel Foote, and Margaret's reputation for outlandish behaviour spread far and wide.

During one shopping trip a fellow traveller in her carriage was terrified to see what she thought was an adder slithering out of one of Margaret's pockets. Quite unperturbed Margaret went on to calm the hysterical woman and simply remarked that her purchases had included several eels, one of them 'alive and sprawling'. During another holiday at Scarborough she asked her coachman and then her footman to carry a pie to be cooked at the local bakehouse. Both servants declined as they considered it to be beneath their dignity, so Margaret's solution was to order her carriage. Attended by coachman and footman, she took her usual place and carried the pie all the way to the bakehouse door from the comfort of her carriage seat. She used the same means to bring the baked pie home.

Late in life Margaret Wharton befriended a clergyman's widow who lived in Thirsk with her four daughters. Arriving there with her carriage and servants she decided to stay on, although her host was unhappy with the arrangement. An appeal to Margaret's nephew at Skelton proved unsuccessful and, rather than see her return to the family home, he arranged to pay her long-suffering host £200 a year during his aunt's lifetime and £100 for each year that she outlived her.

Margaret Wharton died at Thirsk at the age of one hundred and three, outliving her nephew, John Hall Stevenson, whose eccentricities have already been touched on.

JOHN WRIGHTSON

During the late eighteenth and early nineteenth centuries many people's lives were governed by a range of superstitions, belief in witchcraft and fear of unpredictable supernatural phenomena. Such an atmosphere of fear and uncertainty often produced locally based wise men, and North Yorkshire's best-known practitioner of patent cures and all-round counselling was John Wrightson.

Moving to Stokesley from Sedgefield, he advertised under the title of the 'seventh son of a seventh son' while offering to provide advice and cures for both human and animal conditions. Customers called on Wrightson's 'powers' to solve crimes, to resolve emotional or family problems, remove curses cast by local witches and predict future events, as well as to heal diseased livestock. In order to add authority to his claims, John Wrightson dressed the part with flowing robe and printed hat while clutching his crystal ball and making reference to sizeable tomes.

Stokesley High Street. John Wrightson, magician and eccentric, was based in the town for several years.

Much of Wrightson's success has been put down to a network of spies who fed back details of local goings-on and, although it seems that he had a thorough knowledge of herbs and drugs, a major factor must have been the ignorance and gullibility of contemporary North Yorkshire folk.

Eventually John Wrightson was exposed as a fraudster and moved away from Stokesley in 1808 to ply his dubious trade in the Malton area. For a number of years he revived his career as a conman but during 1818 the forces of law caught up with him and he was sentenced to a term of detention in Northallerton prison. Rather than face the prospect of imprisonment, Wrightson took poison as the black maria passed through Hovingham and brought to an end his colourful life as a conman.

JAMES LOWTHER

The Wilton estates, near Redcar, have endured a chequered history since ownership was given to the Bulmer family during the twelfth

9

Wilton Castle, home of James Lowther.

century. An early residence was fortified to withstand Scottish raiding parties, and in the mid-sixteenth century Sir John Bulmer and his wife were put to death after supporting the northern rebellion known as the Pilgrimage of Grace.

Quieter times returned to North Yorkshire during the early eighteenth century and in 1748 Wilton passed into the ownership of Sir James Lowther. Parts of the Bulmer family's medieval castle had survived until Sir James' arrival but the onset of mental illness brought a decline in the fortunes of both castle buildings and the adjacent estate. In 1777 construction work got under way on an embankment in order to reclaim large areas of tidal flats along the Tees between Cargo Fleet and Warrenby. Work was almost complete when wages for the workforce failed to arrive and the project was abandoned. Soon afterwards the wall was breached during storm tides and within a short time all traces of the embankment had disappeared.

Many of Sir James' later eccentricities, described as 'coloured with superstitious and avaricious displays', can probably be explained by his

Wilton Castle, north front.

declining mental condition. Inheritance of the Wilton estates had
made him an extremely wealthy man but he continued to maintain
that he lived in utter poverty. Payments of parish relief were delivered
to the eccentric earl at his home in Wilton Castle, but when he died in
1802 coinage totalling almost £100,000 was discovered in his
bedroom.

The church of St Eloy, Great Smeaton.

2 Ecclesiastical Curiosities

Church buildings represent one of the most treasured aspects of our national heritage. They are found at the heart of most of our communities, large or small, or in some cases in splendid isolation, far removed from the settlements that they serve. Each one is unique – with different periods of architecture and monuments to local families and individuals encapsulating the history of the local area – but a few churches have features that make them rather different from the rest.

Apart from some fourteenth-century arcades and a splendid Norman font carved with lattice and diamond pattern which the sculptor failed to complete, most of the church of St Eloy at Great Smeaton dates from the 1860s when it was redesigned by George Edmund Street (1824–81). The unique distinction of the church is its dedication to St Eloy, for it is believed that there is no other church in England with the blacksmiths' and metalworkers' saint as patron.

On the other hand, the dedication of the church at Danby Wiske is unknown. A point of particular interest is the Norman south doorway, which has the only tympanum (the area between the lintel of the doorway and the arch above) in North Yorkshire *in situ*. It shows three figures in long robes with one of them handing a square object, probably a book, to a smaller person.

St Hilda's Church, at Danby in Cleveland, is set among glorious moorland scenery some 2 miles from the village of Danby. The tower is medieval but the nave dates from 1789 and the chancel was rebuilt in 1848. Canon John Christopher Atkinson was vicar here from 1847 to 1900 and his recollections in the book *Forty Years in a Moorland Parish* provide a valuable insight into life and work throughout this area of North Yorkshire in the late nineteenth century. Canon Atkinson covered thousands of miles during his ministry at Danby and debate focuses on the reasons for the church's isolated position. There are suggestions that the original village was located near the church before it was abandoned and relocated, while other theories suggest that until the development of the modern village in the late eighteenth and early nineteenth centuries the church building was in a central position to meet the needs of parishioners at surrounding farms.

The church of St Mary the Virgin at Leake stands in splendid isolation, with only Leake Hall for company, on the east side of the A19 some 15 miles south of Teesside. The tower and arcades in the nave date from the Norman period while the rest of this fine building dates from the thirteenth and fourteenth centuries. Some splendid woodwork includes two sixteenth-century stalls that were carved in 1519 by the noted school of Ripon carvers and brought here from Bridlington Priory, and seventeenth-century benches, communion rails and font cover. Yet the question usually posed by passers-by relates to

The church of St Mary the Virgin, Leake, set in splendid isolation beside the southbound A19.

The chancel of Leake Church.

the whereabouts of the village. Local folklore throws up a Danish connection, probably prompted by the name of a track behind the hall, 'Dane's Lane', which suggests that the invaders were wiped out by local women who rose in rebellion. In 1852 the discovery of a pit containing the remains of about 500 people added weight to this claim but other sources offer plague, Scottish raiders or change of land use for sheep farming as alternative reasons for the disappearance of any early settlement.

The same factors may have accounted for the disappearance of a possible settlement at nearby Over Silton where the church of St Mary is located in the middle of fields some distance from the village. Much

St Mary's Church, Over Silton.

of the building dates from the Norman period with the addition of a bellcote in the fourteenth century and an east window during the fifteenth. Earthworks in the field on the west side of the church suggest that there was once a thriving village adjacent to St Mary's (south-east of the contemporary settlement).

During the later decades of the nineteenth century many parts of east Cleveland (between Guisborough and the coast) were transformed by the ironstone boom, with tiny communities growing rapidly to house the workforce of the nearby mines. Typical of these settlements is Skelton in Cleveland, where several new communities (New Skelton, North Skelton and Skelton Green) were built away from the original heart of the village. At the east end of Skelton High Street stands the impressive All Saints' Church, completed in 1884 with an unusual south porch tower. Instead of being incorporated into the main church building, the tower is separated from the west end by a short linking passage.

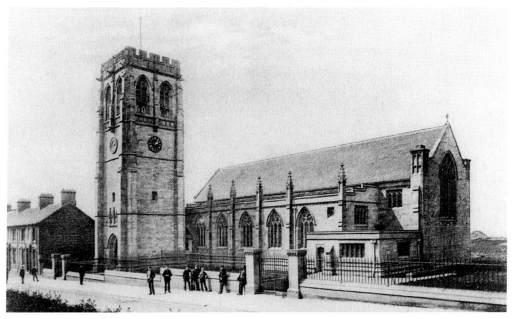

All Saints' Church, Skelton in Cleveland (built 1884).

All Saints' Old Church is set among parkland of the adjacent castle at the west end of Skelton. It is probably the third church on the site and mainly dates from 1785 with furnishings that include pulpit, box pews, west gallery and family pew with a fireplace. Following a thorough programme of restoration work, it is now in the care of the Churches' Conservation Trust.

St Gregory's Church at Bedale is considered by many observers to be among the most outstanding church buildings in North Yorkshire. The spreading nave is filled with light, and fourteenth-century wall paintings are of particular interest, but the most fascinating feature is the early fourteenth-century tower, which is believed to have been built as a place of refuge from border raiders. The three lower sections with small windows date from about 1330 and the top storey is from the fifteenth century. A most unusual and charming feature is the little stone-ribbed porch in the south side, which leads into a vaulted basement. The first floor of the tower incorporates a room with a blocked fireplace, and the

Coxwold Church where Laurence Sterne, friend of John Hall Stevenson,
was vicar for the last eight years of his life. He died in 1768.

doorway at the bottom of the stairs leading to it was protected by a portcullis with grooves between the two arches – still clearly visible.

The picturesque village of Coxwold is well known for its links with Laurence Sterne who was vicar here for eight years up to his death in 1768. He combined his duties as village parson with writing and rural pursuits such as shooting, and it was during his time at Coxwold that Sterne completed *The Life and Opinions of Tristram Shandy* and wrote *A Sentimental Journey*. As a soul-mate of John Hall Stevenson (squire of Skelton Castle) and a member of the Demoniacs Club that met at Skelton, Sterne's behaviour was often eccentric, and it is only fitting that his church at Coxwold should include some dramatic and distinctive features. Much of the building, including the unusual octagonal west tower, dates from the fifteenth century, although the chancel was rebuilt in 1774. This eastern section of the church houses a collection of large, elaborate monuments, mainly commemorating the Bellasis family who lived at nearby Newburgh Priory.

If St Michael's Church at Coxwold is unusual then St Mary's, Whitby, is totally extraordinary. Hovering on the east cliff at the top of 199 stone steps known as Church Stairs, the exterior shows a wonderful mixture of medieval and Georgian styles and has a very striking interior that was remodelled in the eighteenth century. Galleries, box pews and the spreading Cholmley family pew (dating from about 1620) crowd around a three-deck pulpit, which was installed in about 1778. Fixed to the side of the pulpit are ear trumpets, which are said to have been put there by the vicar (between 1809 and 1843) so that his deaf wife, sitting below, could clearly hear his every word. Other unusual features in this amazing building include a rare jade pew, where women who were found guilty of offences such as adultery were dealt with after being dressed in a shroud and walking barefoot to this location, and the model of a Greek temple in the porch which serves as a memorial to victims of the 1861 Lifeboat Disaster.

St Peter's Church at Croft stands close to the road bridge over the River Tees but it has a couple of things in common with St Mary's on the cliff top at Whitby. External walls are a real patchwork of styles and materials and the interior is dominated by a huge family pew. Standing on high oak pillars, it is about 15 feet long and was built shortly before 1680 for the Milbanke family of nearby Halnaby Hall. Access to this incredible structure was via a long spreading staircase with twisted balusters. A curious stone panel close to the doorway that shows a small human figure with one arm raised is said to be Romano-British. Along with the Lewis Carroll connection it adds to the sense of frivolity around the church. Charles Lutwidge Dodgson, better known as Lewis Carroll, spent several years at Croft where his father was rector. The family moved here in 1843 when he was eleven years old and storylines for his world-famous book, *Alice in Wonderland*, are said to have originated during his time in Croft.

There are several contenders in North Yorkshire for the title of the country's smallest church. St Andrew's Old Church at Upleatham is set in rolling countryside on the north side of the Skelton Beck with fine views of east Cleveland's coastal strip. In fact it is only the western end of an earlier Norman church with a tower added in 1684 and, although its future has been called into question from time to time, the fabric has been restored in recent years. St James' Church at Fordon, some 6 miles west of Filey, has a similar background. Standing on a steep bank above the few remaining buildings of a shrunken village, it has been heavily restored but still includes a Norman south doorway along with other Norman items inside the building. Completing this intriguing trio of tiny churches is St Leonard's, at Speeton between Filey and Bridlington. Set in splendid isolation in a field at the top of a cliff, there is stonework from the early Norman period. A carving in the north wall is a twelfth-century Agnus Dei which shows the Lamb of God with a halo and carrying a cross and banner.

Churches often retain an assortment of strange items from earlier times and the Church of All Saints and St John at Easingwold contains a rather grim throwback to the days of extreme poverty. Standing at the west end of this intriguing building – with a drooping gallery and bulging chancel walls – is a communal or parish coffin. The poor of the town were carried to the churchyard on the town's northern edge in the coffin before burial in a shroud. The coffin would then be returned to the church for future use. Metal plates on the side allowed it to be locked so that the corpse could not be stolen by body snatchers. The only other parish coffin to survive to the present day is

St Andrew's Old Church, Upleatham.

to be found at Howden, near Goole, and after a period on loan to the Victoria & Albert Museum, this sombre relic is now back in its rightful place in the church.

The western wall of the churchyard at St Mary's Church, Old Malton, includes a space that served as a coffin rest – with an adjacent plaque giving details of its use in this quiet corner. At Whitby too each year thousands of people make their way up and down the 199 steps and some pause for a while on benches at the side to take in those dramatic views or to regain their breath. How many visitors appreciate that these simple wooden benches are not seats but coffin rests? Bearers could stop briefly on their way to the cliff-top churchyard around St Mary's!

On the subject of coffins, the *North Eastern Daily Gazette* dated 14 March 1883 reported: 'It is said there is a farmer in North

Yorkshire who has hit upon a funny plan to save his heirs the expense of a coffin. He has bought the coffin himself, fitted it up as a cupboard by the side of his bed and is making a good thing by showing it to morbidly curious persons at a penny per head. He raised nearly six shillings in less than half as many days; and by a simple calculation it is made out that, provided the farmer lives long enough, the coffin will earn its own price and the whole of the undertaker's bill.'

St Mary's Church at Old Malton is unusual because it is a dramatic fragment of the Gilbertine Priory that was built on the site by Eustace FitzJohn in the mid-twelfth century. Most of the monastic buildings were demolished soon after 1539 and the central tower disappeared in the mid-seventeenth century. By 1732 more bouts of demolition had reduced the building to its present proportions and since then regular restoration schemes have preserved stonework which includes transitional Norman, early English and Perpendicular styles. Most of the internal furnishings date from the Victorian period, while the roof and organ case were installed during Temple Moore's restoration scheme of 1899–1900.

The pretty village of Lastingham boasts a fine parish church complete with late eleventh-century crypt. Ranking as one of this country's finest examples of its type, the crypt has extremely sturdy Norman columns supporting a vaulted roof and comprises nave, chancel and two side aisles. In fact it was planned as the first stage of an abbey building on the site, but after just ten years at Lastingham the monks, under Abbot Stephen of Whitby, moved to a safer location at York and founded St Mary's Abbey. It seems that plans to turn the embryonic abbey into a parish church were put forward in 1230 and this resulted in an intriguing mixture of Norman and English building styles.

During the eighteenth century the wife of one curate ran the village inn, the Blacksmith's Arms, and the curate himself, Jeremiah Carter, played his fiddle in the pub on Sundays. When hauled before church authorities the young curate, who was father of thirteen children, put up a stout defence and was allowed to continue his ministry in the village.

On the connection between church and inn, the *North Eastern Gazette* for 3 February 1938 reported that the vicarage and the village inn were housed in the same building in the village of Hilton, near

St Mary's Church, Lastingham.

Yarm. The article pointed out that the two homes had separate entrances but from the roadway they gave the impression of being one place. Every Sunday it seems that the vicar emerged from one door while the innkeeper's wife came from a separate door, in the Falcon Inn. At the end of Sunday service both returned to their separate homes in the same building and may well not have met again before the following Sunday.

Mystery surrounds events at the church in Carlton in Cleveland during October 1881. The vicar, the Revd George Sanger, had spent two years, 1878–9, helping to erect a fine new church building, and it opened officially on 13 March 1879. Some two and a half years later, in the early hours of 19 October 1881, fire swept through the church

The crypt of St Mary's Church, Lastingham.

The Falcon Inn, Hilton, formerly part inn and part vicarage.

and suspicion soon focused on the vicar, who was arrested and charged with arson. Sanger was subsequently acquitted by magistrates in Stokesley, but local feelings were running high and the Archbishop of York suspended the vicar for five years. As local folk came forward with evidence against him, Sanger reported incidents of vandalism and harassment and he became an outcast from many of the village folk. It was left to George Sanger's successor as vicar, Canon Kyle, to arrange the construction of a replacement church building and overcome any lingering hostility from parishioners.

Some churches hold particular interest because of rare or unusual features. The church of St Peter and St Paul at Pickering has an

St Botolph's Church, Carlton in Cleveland.

outstanding collection of mid-fifteenth-century wall paintings. Discovered in 1851 after being concealed under whitewash they were restored some thirty years later. The frescoes completely cover the north and south walls of the nave and depict a whole range of biblical scenes from the execution of St John to scenes from the Passion of Our Lord. St Agatha's Church at Easby, near Richmond, has a collection of mid-thirteenth-century paintings.

In the churchyard of All Saints' Church at Ripley is the base of a medieval kneeling, or weeping, cross with eight niches where penitents would have knelt. Outside the south porch of St Mary's Church, Masham, stands the impressive shaft of an Anglo-Saxon cross. Measuring 7 feet in height, it is richly carved with figures representing Our Lord and the twelve apostles and was probably part of an enormous cross that was fashioned more than a thousand years ago.

The interior of the present-day St Botolph's Church, Carlton in Cleveland.

Just outside the north-east part of All Saints' Church at Saxton lies the tomb of Lord Dacre, who died at the Battle of Towton in 1461. It is unusual to find an altar tomb of this age in a churchyard.

Mystery surrounds another tomb or, more accurately, the reputed tomb at Newburgh Priory, which is said to hold the remains of Oliver Cromwell. Most reports claim that Cromwell's remains were dug up after the restoration of King Charles II in 1660 and displayed at Tyburn. However, a long-held belief at Newburgh Priory states that his daughter Mary, Countess of Fauconberg, bribed someone to substitute another corpse for her father's, which she secretly transferred to this curious corner of her husband's family home. Down the years the vault has remained undisturbed, and the mystery surrounding Cromwell's final resting place continues to mystify and intrigue visitors to this charming corner of North Yorkshire.

The Lady Chapel, three-quarters of a mile north of Osmotherley.

There's a similar mystery associated with the Chapel of Our Lady of Mount Grace near Osmotherley. Monks from the nearby Carthusian priory spent recreation days at the chapel, which was granted a licence in 1397 for mass to be said on a regular basis. At times it was used as a hermitage and after the closure of Mount Grace Priory in 1539 the Lady Chapel remained in Catholic hands. Soon after 1832 the chapel passed out of Catholic ownership but local people continued to make pilgrimages especially on Lady Days. Following the death of Sir Maurice Bell of Ingleby Arncliffe in 1942 the chapel was returned to Catholic ownership and pilgrimages increased throughout the year. In 1960 the building was renovated and the official reopening was conducted by Cardinal Godfrey, Archbishop of Westminster. No one knows why hordes of people have made the pilgrimage, at times with the prospect of persecution by the authorities. One theory maintains that Margaret Clitherow was buried here after being crushed to death for the crime of harbouring priests and allowing her home in York's Shambles to be used for celebrating mass, while another suggests that St Cuthbert's remains were secretly transported to this remote North Yorkshire location.

3 Follies

They come in all shapes and sizes. Unusual, sometimes eccentric designs completed at the whim of a rich man as a mere indulgence are perhaps in celebration of an important local or national event . . . but all follies hold a certain fascination.

There are several very different follies in the Richmond area. Aske Hall Temple on Lord Zetland's estate must rank as one of the largest Gothic-style follies in the whole country. With arcading around the ground floor, pointed windows and angle turrets it has many features typical of mid-eighteenth-century early Gothic styling. A staircase at the rear is said to have enabled local merry-makers to come and go without being observed, but a more likely explanation is that its positioning was planned so that it did not affect the overall design work, which has been attributed to Daniel Garrett.

Closer to Richmond, on the east side of the B6274 road, is a folly known as Oliver Duckett. Named after the late eighteenth-century owner, it was later acquired by Sir Conyers Darcy and converted into a solid-looking Gothic folly. A high stone base supports a round tower with gun ports and turrets, with an entrance, reached only by using a ladder, at first floor level.

Culloden Tower is a prominent landmark on the south-western side of Richmond. Standing in an elevated position within the 35-acre estate surrounding Temple Lodge (off Cravengate), it was built in 1747 to celebrate the Yorke family's involvement in the defeat of Jacobite forces just one hundred years earlier (and was originally known as the Cumberland Temple). It is believed that this architect, too, was Daniel Garrett and his plans produced an octagonal structure on a square base (with an additional external staircase). By 1981 Culloden Tower had suffered badly at the hands of vandals and ground floor rooms were in use as a cowshed and haystore. This splendid structure was saved from total dereliction and eventual demolition by the Landmark

Duckett's Folly, Richmond.

Trust, which carried out a thorough restoration of the whole building. Parts of the original tower were painstakingly restored and other aspects were carefully rebuilt using old photographs and fragments of plasterwork. A spiral staircase composed of ninety-eight stone steps winds through four floors from the ground floor bathroom up to the impressive master bedroom on the top floor. A superb first floor chimneypiece and several fine ceilings give this unusual building an overall feeling of charming elegance and, of course, the views across Richmond and its nearby countryside are spellbinding.

The Landmark Trust has also restored and adapted a pigsty near Fyling Hall, Robin Hood's Bay . . . but this is no ordinary pigsty! Built in 1883 by Squire Barry of Fyling Hall, it is positively palatial and boasts a classical frontage. Construction work is said to have taken three men some two years because of the eccentric squire's constant

Culloden Tower, Richmond.

changes of mind about its design. Perhaps this accounts for Doric columns across the façade and distinctly Egyptian-looking windows at the rear, but there's no denying that the coastal views away to the south are quite stunning.

From pigsty to palace . . . well, at least the stately piles of landed families where a whole variety of classical-style structures were added to swathes of North Yorkshire's landscape. In 1699 Charles Howard, 3rd Earl of Carlisle, commissioned the soldier and aspiring playwright Sir John Vanbrugh to design and build a suitably grand family home.

Pigsty close to Fyling Hall, Robin Hood's Bay.

With assistance from Nicholas Hawksmoor, the results of Vanbrugh's labours are quite remarkable, with a series of buildings enhancing approaches to the main palace. Two spectacular gateways give access to the estate. The Carrmire Gate with its castellated walls and brick pyramids and the Pyramid Gate, which includes eleven different Gothic bastions, provide a dramatic introduction to the estate. To the east of the main house is the Temple of the Four Winds, which imitates the style of Palladio's Villa Rotonda. Set on a simple stone-walled platform it has a central dome with octagonal windows on a square body, while ornate vases, busts and Ionic columns complete the overall charm.

Views from the temple take in Sion Wood, the three-arched New River Bridge and, as a focal point, the huge mausoleum. Designed by Hawksmoor in 1728, work began in 1731 but was only completed in

Temple of the Four Winds, Castle Howard.

1742 after his death. Beneath the dome a frieze encircles the surrounding walls, which enclose the family vault where the 3rd Earl is buried.

Duncombe Park at Helmsley has fewer grand buildings than Castle Howard but the overall landscaping scheme ranks as one of the finest in the whole of Britain. It is the natural beauty of the Rye Valley that really catches the eye but both the Duncombe Terrace (east of the main house) and Rievaulx Terrace (3 miles to the west overlooking Rievaulx Abbey) have classical-style temples at either end of long grassy expanses. The discovery of stonework in the valley between the two terraces has prompted some historians to suggest that plans were prepared to connect the terraces with the temples.

The Turner family estate at Kirkleatham, near Redcar, included a hall, free school or old hall building, stable block and whole series of

Mausoleum, Duncombe Park, Helmsley.

ornamental features on sloping ground to the south. John Turner bought the estate in 1623 and his son built the original hall, which was remodelled along with the surrounding estate in the mid-eighteenth century.

Sadly, most of the ornamental 'follies' including an ice house, 'Neptune's pool', a temple or pavilion with Gothic windows and internal Rococo plasterwork and a Gothic-style pigeon-cote, complete with arrow loops, towers and castellation, have all disappeared along with the hall (demolished in 1956). Tantalising glimpses of former glories survive in the form of an ornamental arch and circular turrets or 'bastions', which represented part of the defences around the gardens.

Many follies blend well into their natural surroundings but some look distinctly out of place. Unlike Ravenscar, which never developed as a resort, Saltburn-by-the-Sea took shape on a greenfield site during the 1860s and '70s and, although the original plan around a central Regent Circus was not carried through, the sparkling new township included many attractions for the hordes of late Victorian visitors. One feature, however, did seem a little out of place. Prince Albert, husband of Queen Victoria, died of typhoid in 1861 and three years later a memorial was planned for the developing resort. The portico of Barnard Castle's railway station was brought to Saltburn and the cost of resiting it in the pleasure gardens was estimated at £300. Saltburn Improvement Committee was unable to push ahead at the time and it was 1867 before Shaftoe and Barry of York were given the work, which cost £100. The porch, which included two pairs of Corinthian columns, was given a rear wall with semicircular recess when it was installed in a prominent position high above Skelton Beck.

Even more amazing than the Albert Memorial in its unlikely location is the sight of an imitation Stonehenge near the village of Ilton, west of Masham. It was the brainchild of an eccentric writer, William Danby (1752–1833) who produced a number of books with the titles, *Travelling Thoughts*, then *Thoughts Chiefly on Serious Subjects* and *Thoughts on Various Subjects*. He also had great humanity and came up with an unlikely scheme to create work for unemployed local men. Members of the assembled workforce were paid a shilling each day as they laboured on the scheme to re-create an incredible collection of columns, altars and standing stones. Set in the middle of Forestry Commission land, there are fine views away to the west across Leighton Reservoir.

One of the smallest follies to be found anywhere in the country stands proudly on a garden wall in West Street, Yarm. Several cement model buildings collectively make up Yarm Castle and were the work of eighteen-year-old David Doughty, who lived in the adjacent Commondale House during the 1880s. The central feature, a typical

Perimeter feature of the Druids Temple at Ilton.

'Stonehenge'.

The column of stones a short distance from the main temple area.

Yarm Castle, West Street, Yarm.

keep, stands 2 feet high, and includes more than 800 windows which could be illuminated from inside by gas on important occasions. A 'town hall', which stands alongside the castle, was added by Doughty's son Henry, and there are other examples of David Doughty's skills in cement model making in the rear garden. These include a model abbey ruin, two medieval knights in full armour and an Egyptian-style screen.

4 Failed Schemes

The Victorian era is renowned for spectacular civil engineering or industrial projects and an impressive programme of public works. Fortunes were made alongside worldwide reputations but amid the dramatic success stories are scattered any number of failed schemes that often left speculators and promoters regretting their bouts of over-ambition and financial gambles.

A rapidly expanding railway network was the key to much of Britain's nineteenth-century growth and facilitated dramatic social and economic changes. One direct result of this spreading programme of rail development was an ending of the period of 'canal mania' that had swept the country a few decades earlier.

Some canal schemes never progressed beyond the earliest planning stages and were usually abandoned on account of prohibitive costs, but in other cases building work got under way. Plans were prepared in the mid-1730s to make the rivers Ouse and Swale navigable as far as the higher reaches at Morton Bridge and Bedale but, like many other similar proposals, they were not followed up. Three decades later the situation had changed dramatically as a programme of canal building swept the country. The scheme was revived and after surveys had been completed application was made for an Act of Parliament. Similar parliamentary moves were made for schemes on the Ure at Boroughbridge and Ripon and along the Cod Beck at Thirsk.

John Smith was appointed as engineer for building work on the Ouse as well as the Swale and progress was made during summer 1768 in spite of a constant battle with high water levels. Topcliffe Lock was opened on 25 January 1769 and almost exactly seven months later, on 24 August, Linton Lock opened for business. Work on the Ure and Ripon Canal was finished before long but it was a different story at the market towns of Thirsk and Bedale.

Bedale 'Harbour' basin for barges on the proposed canal.

Following parliamentary approval in 1767 for work along the Cod Beck, a wharf was constructed close to Finkle Street Bridge as well as a lock some 400 yards downstream on low-lying ground known as the Flatts. As financial support for the scheme dwindled away the facilities were never used by vessels and the lock was converted into a bridge. Similar problems affected the scheme that was intended to link Bedale to the Swale and Ouse. At the southern end of the town a substantial weir crosses Bedale Beck and impressive stonewalls along the bank form what was intended to be a canal basin. Known locally as 'The Harbour' it was constructed in the late 1760s as a loading area for

Cod Beck on the south side of Thirsk, where wharves were constructed
for the canal.

vessels travelling via the Swale and Ouse. Iron mooring rings in the
walls were never used, and with the scheme floundering through lack
of financial backing, it was finally abandoned when the Bedale–
Leyburn branch railway reached the town in 1855.

The era of canal building was brought to an end by the rapid
expansion of railway networks, and north-eastern engineers such as
Timothy Hackworth, George and Robert Stephenson and Matthew
Murray played leading roles in locomotive and civil engineering
schemes. Railways originated as tramways linking coalmines with
river systems in the north-east, and railways also played a crucial role
in exploitation of ironstone deposits in North Yorkshire. In many
locations it is still possible to identify cuttings, embankments and
bridges that carried mineral lines from mines to the major rail routes,
but the most curious of all these lines was the Cleveland Mineral
Extension Railway. Better known as Paddy Waddell's Railway, it had an

eventful lifespan and goes down in history as the railway that never was.

Promoter of the line was Joseph Dodds from Winston, near Darlington, and subscribers to the scheme included Carl Bolckow and Lord Downe. The plan was to transport ironstone from mines in the East Cleveland area around Skelton and Brotton across the moors for about 10 miles to ironworks at Glaisdale in the Esk Valley. Initial moves to gain parliamentary approval were halted by promoters of a line between Whitby and Loftus, and although the Glaisdale ironworks had opened in 1866 it was the summer of 1873 before the bill was given royal assent. Joseph Dodds was the central figure at a ceremonial turf cutting held in the remote village of Moorsholm, and the line's engineer was John Waddell whose other projects included London's Putney Bridge, the Mersey Rail Tunnel and the Whitby–Loftus and Whitby–Scarborough railways. John Waddell's nickname, 'Paddy', may have originated from the hordes of Irish navvies who carried out heavy manual work on his engineering projects.

After the impetus of the ceremony at Moorsholm and completion of a prominent yellow brick railway hotel in the village the scheme ran into severe difficulties. Financial backing for ongoing construction work did not materialise, and as the project faltered 'revival' acts had to be obtained in 1878 and 1881. Periods of activity followed by inaction brought a total of seven acts sanctioning building work on the line through to 1896.

Apart from the impressive but incongruous railway hotel at Moorsholm (which was demolished in the mid-1990s) there are several other reminders of this ill-fated project. Cottages close to Glaisdale and Lealholm served as temporary inns for construction workers, and embankments and a cutting on either side of the A171 road, west of Scaling Dam, mark the line of the route. With hindsight, it seems surprising that backing for the scheme, intermittent as it was, continued for such a long period of time. The dramatic era of mid-nineteenth-century railway building was coming to an end when promoters attempted to raise capital, and closure of the ironworks at Glaisdale in 1876 might have signalled the death knell of the whole scheme. Severe and long-lasting depression hit the iron trade during the 1880s and, although the final deadline for completion of work

The former Station Hotel, Boosbeck, serving Paddy Waddell's Railway
(demolished late 1990s).

only lapsed in 1896, the railway was doomed. It seems only appropriate that such a protracted, ambitious and unfinished scheme should find a place in local industrial history, and indeed folklore, as the railway that never was.

The same industrial problems that affected Paddy Waddell's Railway in the 1880s also caused social and economic distress throughout North Yorkshire's ironstone mining area and left a fine new school at Kilton Thorpe empty and unused. Located some 2 miles from Carlin How and Brotton, the community grew up around the ironstone mine that was opened by Kilton Iron Company in 1875. With an anticipated influx of miners and their families three rows of thirty houses were constructed, as well as the school buildings. Desks, blackboards and books were installed in the schoolroom but no pupils ever arrived for lessons. A strike among ironstone miners was followed by recession, and the building remained unused apart from staging a wedding reception. It had no running water or drainage and, although the adjacent schoolmaster's house became a domestic residence, the schoolroom was only used as a forestry store. Empty houses in the tiny community remained unoccupied and were eventually demolished while the school became increasingly overgrown and dilapidated. Kilton mine closed in 1963 and the roofless, red brick school building with pointed church-like windows was left open to the elements until the mid-1990s when it was tastefully restored as a private residence.

Nineteenth-century railway development gave a major boost to seaside resorts around the country and major venues such as Brighton, Blackpool and Scarborough all benefited from new-fangled rail links with inland conurbations. In addition to Scarborough, several other North Yorkshire resorts such as Filey, Bridlington, Whitby and Hornsea continue to attract crowds of holidaymakers but there is little evidence of a grand plan for another major holiday location at Ravenscar.

Until the 1770s Ravenscar was a scattered collection of farm buildings close to the cliff tops between Whitby and Scarborough. Captain William Childs took over ownership of local alum mines in 1763 and some eleven years later he built Raven Hall on the site of a Roman fort, as a family holiday retreat. On his death in 1829 the hall passed to the Willis family and it was then bought by Mr William

Kilton Thorpe tip, adjacent to the ironstone mine and 'school that never was'.

Kilton Thorpe school and school house (the building has recently been restored as a private residence).

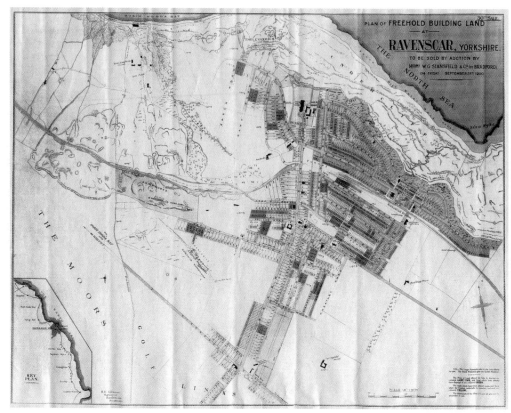

Ravenscar, 'the resort that never was'. Plan for the cliff top township.

Hammond during 1845. As a director of the Scarborough to Whitby railway line, Mr Hammond was instrumental in routing the track through Ravenscar, but he died a few months before the line was completed in 1885. When his wife died five years later the property was inherited by four daughters and they promptly sold it to the Peak Estate Company for development as a holiday resort. The central figure in the company was John Septimus Bland. An ambitious scheme was drawn up, spread across 750 acres of land between the cliff top and the Scarborough–Whitby road. At the heart of the planned resort was the railway station with a total of 1,200 building plots ranged along

Perimeter wall of the Raven Hall Hotel, Ravenscar.

wide roadways with names such as Marine Esplanade and Cliff Road, while the area's historical links were echoed in Roman Road, Dane Road and Saxon Road. A workforce numbering between three and four hundred was brought in to carry out building work and the company opened their own brickyard in the locality to provide materials. As the construction programme got under way roads and basic services were installed and building plots were advertised for sale at an average cost of £80. Few of the sites were sold and, in addition to a row of shops and hotel near the station, the new resort gained only about a dozen residences. Inevitably, perhaps, the Peak Estate Company was declared bankrupt in the 1920s and the whole project collapsed, leaving contemporary commentators to dub this windy clifftop setting 'the town that never was'.

Ravenscar's unused railway platform, August 2002.

Raven Hall Hotel, Ravenscar.

The swirling mists that bedevilled plans for a resort at Ravenscar in the late nineteenth century had fuelled calls for a harbour of refuge at Redcar some seventy years earlier. Along with biting north-east gales, foggy conditions were the main cause of shipping losses down the north Yorkshire coast and by the 1830s proposals were put forward for an ambitious scheme that would offer vessels a safe haven. In 1832 an engineer from Stockton on Tees, W.A. Brookes, prepared plans that would create a large natural harbour covering some 500 acres within parallel ridges of rock (Salt Scar and East Scar) that ran into the sea from the foreshore. Depth of water at the entrance would be 5 fathoms.

As the scheme progressed a management committee was set up, and royal approval was granted to call the planned harbour 'Port William'. There was strong support from sea-going men who maintained that such an area of enclosed deep water would offer the best safe refuge between Yarmouth (in East Anglia) and Leith (in Scotland). Further weight was added to the case during the early months of 1835 when more than thirty vessels, of which fourteen were total losses, foundered in Tees Bay, but the stumbling block, as so often is the case, was the huge cost of construction work. Estimates in the region of £300,000 proved to be prohibitive although supporters argued that the projected harbour would have saved its cost in sailing ships, not to mention human life. Slag from the growing number of furnaces along the banks of the Tees was dumped in the sea off South Gate, instead of along the ridges of the Salt Scar and East Scar Rocks, and the Redcar lifeboat, *Zetland* – built in 1800 – continued in service until 1880 when it was credited with having saved 502 lives. The grand scheme that might have transformed Redcar's shoreline with an impressive harbour of refuge and at the same time opened up fishing and tourism opportunities never got beyond the detailed planning stages.

THE BRIDGE THAT NEVER WAS

Every day thousands of motorists cross the River Tees on the old stone bridge between Yarm and Eaglescliffe but few appreciate that it should have disappeared long ago. Parts of the structure date from around AD 1400 when Walter Skirlaw, Bishop of Durham, gave orders for building work to get under way. Down the centuries it has taken a battering not only from road traffic but also from rival forces during the English Civil War of the 1640s, and by the late eighteenth century it was seen as unsuited to serve the needs of an increasing volume of traffic. The carriageway was only 12 feet wide and plans were prepared for a splendid single span iron bridge – costing about £8,000.

Work on the new bridge was finished by the end of September 1805 but legal complications meant that it remained unopened. During building work the scheme had been altered so that the actual bridge was 4 feet higher than originally planned and this meant raising the roadway on the Yorkshire bank for about 100 yards. Local residents refused to meet the additional cost and North Riding authorities were unable to charge a rate to cover the extra expenditure before the following year.

Yarm Bridge. The early fifteenth-century road bridge was to be replaced by an iron bridge, but after the collapse of the new structure the original bridge was retained and widened.

IRON.

TO BE SOLD
By Auction,
(BY Mr. KINGSTON,)

On THURSDAY the 2d. day of APRIL, 1807, at the Bridge Ware house in Yarm, in the county of York, in Lots, for the accommodation of purchasers,

About two Tons of malleable Iron.

Also the Blocks, Ropes, &c. lately used in weighing, &c. the Cast Iron of Yarm Bridge.

*** The Sale to begin at 2 o'Clock in the afternoon.

N. B. The Iron must be paid for on delivery; and for particulars, enquire at MESSRS CLARKE & GREY'S Office, in STOCKTON

W. ... Appleton, Printers, Stockton.

A poster advertising scrap iron from Yarm's ill-fated bridge.

An artist's impression of Yarm's 'bridge that never was'.

The impasse was broken at about midnight on 12 January 1806 when the bridge's ironwork crashed into the river below. Daylight clearly showed that the south abutment had collapsed and a group of architects was set up to report on the incident. No blame was attached to Walkers of Rotherham, the company that cast the iron arch, and the main cause was stated to be the fact that the south abutment had been filled with rubble rather than solid stonework. Rather than attempting to rebuild the iron bridge, the decision was taken to widen and strengthen the old stone bridge, and ironwork from the ill-fated bridge was sold off as scrap. During 1908 a single girder from the bridge was hauled out of the Tees by George Goldie, landlord of the nearby Blue Bell Inn, and displayed in the bar.

5 Hills, Horses & Holes in the Ground

The North Yorkshire landscape has a multitude of unusual features that have prompted an endless number of unlikely stories. While some settings are certainly the result of human activity, others are widely regarded as being entirely natural, and in some cases the debate continues.

Several summits on the North York Moors have found their way into the realms of folklore. Blakey Topping has been linked with the legendary giant Wade, who is said to have dumped excess soil from prodigious building projects at this location to create the 800-feet high rounded hilltop that we see today, while Whorl Hill's darkly wooded slopes (on the east side of the A172 near Stokesley) are said to have been the lair of the fearsome Sexhow Worm.

The rounded summit of Freebrough Hill rises to a height of 821 feet above Moorsholm Moor (close to the A171, Guisborough to Whitby road) and stimulates endless discussion about its history. Its symmetrical outlines have led many people to speculate that it is manmade like Silbury Hill in Wiltshire, and there is evidence of Victorian excavations close to the top, but geologists have established that it is a completely natural feature. Layers of rock and boulder clay match those found in the adjacent landscape. This prominent natural landmark seems to have been a rallying point for early settlers as surrounding moorland boasts a whole range of Bronze Age earthworks including groups of barrows, mounds and an enclosure. Several centuries later raiders from northern Europe settled in the area and formed the Kingdom of Deira. The name of the hill is derived from Freya, their goddess of fertility.

Shooting lodge on the northern slope of Roseberry Topping.

Roseberry Topping from Newton under Roseberry.

Roseberry Topping is probably Yorkshire's best-known hill. Its craggy summit has not only been battered by the elements but also by workmen quarrying sandstone, jet and ironstone, and it now stands at about 1,057 feet above sea level. As with Freebrough Hill, so Roseberry attracted early settlers and in 1826 a quarryman unearthed prehistoric items including knives, axe-heads and a gouge, which may be linked with a series of pits and an early settlement on the lower slopes. Its name may originate from the days of Viking raiders and the earliest references to 'Othensberg' and 'Ohensberg' could indicate a link to Odin, the Scandinavian god. Perhaps it should be no surprise that Roseberry Topping has featured in local rhymes, dialect poems and dramatic productions, and down the years its slopes have supported a hermitage, bathing pool and summerhouse that still stands on a ridge above Newton Wood. A plaque on the tiny structure

Roseberry Topping from the south.

informs us that it was built for Commodore Wilson of Ayton Hall in the late eighteenth century. The saddest story linked with Roseberry Topping concerns a Northumbrian princess and her baby son in the Viking era. During a dream the princess had a warning that her child would drown and moved with him to the apparent safety of Roseberry's high ground, but as she slept the infant crept away and was drowned in a nearby well.

With a background history featuring agriculture and field sports it is highly appropriate that the North Yorkshire landscape should display a hillside representation of a white horse. Spreading across the south-facing slope above the village of Kilburn is Britain's most northerly depiction of a 'chalk horse'. It is believed that the scheme was first proposed in the early nineteenth century, with the White Horse of Uffington, Berkshire, as the inspiration, but the work of carving out the huge outline and spreading lime across the surface was completed in the early days of 1857 by John Hodgson, the village schoolmaster, and

The White Horse of Kilburn.

The Hole of Horcum between Pickering and Whitby.

up to thirty-three other local menfolk. The horse's dimensions are dramatic, with a length of 314 feet and height totalling 228 feet while the impact of erosion and a battering from the elements necessitates regular maintenance and repair work. This work is carried out by the Kilburn White Horse Association. Following a major restoration scheme during the 1960s improvements were made to steps on the east side of the horse in 1976, allowing a walk through varying landscapes from Sutton Bank Visitor Centre along the Cleveland Way, and returning through forestry plantations at the foot of the slopes.

The north country has any number of hollows, holes, fissures and openings among the varied landscapes but perhaps the most impressive is the Hole of Horcum, a large natural amphitheatre adjacent to the A169 between Pickering and Whitby. Local folklore suggests that this fine natural bowl was formed by the giant Wade or by the Devil as a punchbowl but the truth is that it has been shaped by the long-term erosive effects of moorland springs.

Saltergate Inn near the 'Devil's Elbow' and the Hole of Horcum.

On a smaller scale, the North York Moors have large numbers of man-made pits scattered across open ground at several locations. There are lines of pits near the Hole of Horcum and others close to Goathland and from the eastern side of Roseberry Topping across Hutton Moor to Highcliff near Guisborough, but the most prominent avenues of pits are from a double line across Easington Moor. Measuring almost 3 feet in depth and 7 feet across they cross open moorland on the south side of Scaling Dam (close to the A171 road). Expert opinion remains divided about the origins and purpose of the pits, with some suggesting that they relate to mining operations or early settlements while others claim a link with military works. Dating the pits has proved equally difficult and the only area of agreement is that they were constructed between the end of the Bronze Age and the later stages of the medieval period.

6 Heavenly Bodies & Weird Weather

B ritish weather must be everyone's most popular topic of conversation. Changeable, unpredictable, depressing . . . always a talking point with friend or stranger and yet every so often even those astonishing skies produce something out of the ordinary. Meteorologists and astronomers can usually explain unusual phenomena but in earlier times it was a different story and harvest failures were blamed on portents in the sky. As a late seventeenth-century chronicler recorded, 'In this month [December 1680] about the eighteenth day, appeared a mighty dreadful comet or blazing star, about north west, and continued all winter, to the amazement of many people, it being of so great length and breadth, and the summer after was a most terrible drought, and great scarcity of hay and grass. . . .'

On 18 August 1783 there were reports from many parts of this country, including North Yorkshire, about an 'extraordinary meteor' which lit up the evening sky to such an extent that shop boards could be read from across the road during the hours of darkness.

More strange heavenly sightings made headlines in the 1820s. Witness accounts on 30 March 1826 gave details of 'a remarkable electrical phenomenon, which was observed between 8 and 10 this evening, consisting of a broad zone of white light, forming an exact arch across the sky. It appeared from the west as a streaming light which passed between the two stars in Orion's shoulder and sweeping through the zenith, it proceeded through the tail of Ursa Major and a little to the north of Cornea Borealis. . . . Its greatest breadth appeared to be four or five degrees. The light was steady and regular, resembling the tail of a comet. . . .'

A similar night-time light show took place some two and a half years later, on 29 September 1828, when contemporary sightings spoke of:

A luminous arch that appeared across the heavens in a direction nearly north east and south west. It was first seen about 7.00 pm issuing from dark clouds near the horizon, quite across the zenith where it intersected the Milky Way to the opposite horizon. Its width continued uniform for some time, being about 3 degrees. The greater part of the sky was clear and thickly studded with stars, which were quite visible through the arch. It remained perfectly steady for some time, and then assumed the fleeting, shadowy nature of the Aurora Borealis. The light in the northern horizon, which had not been remarkable, suddenly, brightened into a most vivid and sublime exhibition of the Aurora, the brilliant streamers of which extended nearly to the zenith. The arch, which had disappeared, again became visible, extending in a direction parallel to its former one, but much further south. The evening was fair and several flying stars shot across the heavens during the continuance of these appearances.

Extreme gale force winds, huge hailstones during midsummer and even minor whirlwinds are not uncommon in parts of the North Country, but the night sky of 12 April 1900 provided a very rare spectacle. A police officer noted the incident in his diary: 'At 2.00 a.m. I saw a lunar rainbow. I was near Broomlands (Cambridge Road, Middlesbrough) at the time and could see it from end to end. The colours were not plain but different colours were discernible.'

There were reports of an earthquake at Whitby on 19 April 1754: 'at about 11.00 p.m.; not only the whole town but also ships in the harbour were affected with it', and similar incidents on 10 March 1843 and 6 October 1863, and it could have been an earth tremor on 14 February 1868 that produced 'a tide of extraordinary magnitude'. The unusual phenomenon appears to have prevailed from the 'Tyne to the Thames and extensive damage to shipping and other property has unfortunately resulted from the great overflow of water'.

Most heavenly bodies remain in the firmament and falls of meteorites are rare. A total of twenty-two meteorites have been known

Railway workers pose beside the hole created by a meteorite near Ormesby.
(*Yorkshire Museum photograph*)

to fall on the British Isles but the North Country has seen two such
incidents in little over two centuries. On 13 December 1795 a
meteorite crashed to the ground close to the east Yorkshire village of
Wold Newton, and less than a hundred years later there was a
similarly dramatic episode on the southern outskirts of Middlesbrough.
There were clear skies on 14 March 1881 when a sonic boom echoed
overhead and within seconds a group of railway workers at
Pennyman's siding (close to Ormesby station) heard a 'rushing or
roaring sound' followed by a thudding noise. About 50 yards away
they came across 'a round vertical hole into which a man's arm might

Railway workers with the meteorite pose alongside the hole next to the railway
track near Ormesby. (*Yorkshire Museum photograph*)

be thrust'. The report by Alexander Herschel, Professor of Physics at
the University of Durham College of Physical Science at Newcastle,
continued: 'Minutes after the fall they withdrew an object from about
30 cm depth finding it now milk warm.' Expert opinion decided that it
must have warmed up as it bored into the railway embankment
because meteorites are normally quite cold on landing. The process of
re-entry through the atmosphere at a speed of 15 miles per second
usually results in a coarse lumpy object but the Middlesbrough
meteorite is rather different. A series of smooth curving channels and
a distinct cone shape resulted from the direction of its re-entry: it

travelled nose-first like a modern space module, rather than twisting and turning as was more usual.

Victorian scientists immediately appreciated the importance of the Middlesbrough meteorite and with Professor Herschel taking a leading role detailed investigations were carried out. Even the hole and surrounding materials were carefully removed and preserved in a box. Several places, including the British Museum, wanted to add this unusual item to their collections and Professor Herschel coordinated discussions on the future of the meteorite. He took advice from Neville Story-Maskelyne MP, a former Professor of Mineralogy at Oxford University and keeper of mineralogy at the British Museum, but in September 1881 the board of the North Eastern Railway ruled that it should be presented to the Yorkshire Philosophical Society, based at the Yorkshire Museum in the city of York. A small portion was removed for closer analysis and copies of the original shell-like object (which measures about 5 inches by 6 inches with a height of close to 3 inches and weighing around 3½ pounds) were sent to other museums, but this amazing object from outer space is still safely housed in the Yorkshire Museum.

7 Of Great Proportions

Every area has its quota of giant stories and North Yorkshire has several such tales. Some belong firmly in the realms of folklore, in others facts and fanciful fable have become mixed, and every so often we come across a genuine real-life character of enormous proportions.

Giant stories involving one-eyed ogres at Sessay, near Thirsk, and at Dalton Mill, close to Topcliffe, have echoes of the pantomime *Jack and the Beanstalk*, where thoroughly unpleasant characters of monstrous size are dispatched by a brave local youth. It was a similar story at Penhill, in Wensleydale, where resistance to a cruel and vengeful giant was led by the local hermit and good inevitably triumphed over evil.

In the case of Wade, a real-life character becomes mixed up with local folklore and is credited with some incredible feats. Wade was an important Saxon leader who lived in the Mulgrave area (near Whitby) and, in AD 794, during the turbulent pre-Norman period, he is said to have killed a rival Northumbrian chieftain named Ethelred. As hostilities between northern leaders dragged on Wade was defeated in battle at Whalley, Lancashire, during 798, and returned to Mulgrave where he died from his injuries. A prominent standing stone in a field near East Barnby has traditionally been said to mark his final resting place – but departing from these few biographical facts, Wade's reputation soon took on enormous dimensions.

Perhaps Wade's status as a giant originates from the fact that there were originally two stones at the East Barnby location. They were set 12 feet apart and were said to indicate his actual height. Another set of stones at nearby Goldsborough were 100 feet apart and promoted even more outrageous claims! Folklore goes on to credit Wade, and his equally outsized wife Bell, with a series of feats, including construction of the castles at Mulgrave and Pickering. During building work, so the

Mulgrave motte and bailey castle was the work of the giant Wade, according to local folklore.

Mulgrave's medieval castle, home of the de Mauley family, linked at times in folklore with the giant Wade.

Mulgrave (medieval) castle was extensively rebuilt in the late 1990s.

The third castle within the Mulgrave estates was built by the Duchess of Buckingham in the 1730s, extended during the late eighteenth century and again in 1814.

story runs, they owned only one heavy hammer and hurled it backwards and forwards across the moors between each site.

Another important man-made feature of the North York Moors is Wade's Causeway, which can be followed for over a mile across Wheeldale Moor near Goathland. Some 16 feet wide and more than a mile long, it has been identified by historians as a section of Roman roadway that linked the area around Malton with coastal bases near Whitby. Folklore tells rather a different tale by suggesting that Wade and Bell built the route either to link their two castles or for Bell to reach her giant cow on the moor tops. The whole story has taken a different turn in recent times as a group of archaeologists have claimed that the roadway is not a Roman route and may well be much

Wade's Causeway on Wheeldale Moor, near Goathland. According to folklore it was the work of the legendary giant Wade, but until recently historians have maintained that it is a Roman road. This theory is now in question.

earlier in origin. Whatever the truth, no one is suggesting that Wade's Causeway is in any way linked with the legendary giant.

In more recent times North Yorkshire has produced a genuine giant. Harry Cooper was born in 1857, probably at Swainby, where he worked as a boy at Scugdale Hall Farm. A directory of 1890 states that 'this remarkable sample of humanity grew 13 inches in the space of five months' and when fully mature his hands measured 13 inches in length and his feet extended an amazing 17 inches. Leaving his work on the farm he then worked at ironstone mines in East Cleveland, including North Skelton mine, but his height of 8 feet 6 inches made him quite unsuitable for any form of manual work.

Henry Cooper, a genuine giant of a man from Scugdale.

Remarkably, Cooper worked in the cramped confines of North Skelton mine before joining the circus.

Harry Cooper soon became known as the 'Yorkshire Giant' and when a circus arrived in Brotton he was persuaded to join the travelling show. He toured Britain with great success and was spotted by the famous Barnum and Bailey Circus, which took him across the Atlantic. During the 1880s he toured the USA and became a major celebrity, as shown in his prominent position at the Circus World Museum in Wisconsin, USA.

North Skelton mine.

A wealth of 'tall' stories grew up around Harry Cooper. Visitors to the circus often posed for photographers beside him but although the intention was to highlight Harry's immense stature, more often than not he sat down for the photographic sessions. It is claimed that contemporary photographers could not fit everyone into the plate if Cooper remained standing! During his time in Britain reports suggest that Harry Cooper was so tall that he used to light his pipe from street gaslights and, as his reputation grew throughout America, he became known as Sir Henry Alexander Cooper or Colonel H.A. Cooper.

It is known that Harry married during his time in USA but there is no record of his wife's height or whether they had any children. His remarkable life came to an end at the age of forty-one in Calgary, Canada, when he weighed 29 stones, and his place in the record books is assured – as the world's tallest man during the Victorian age.

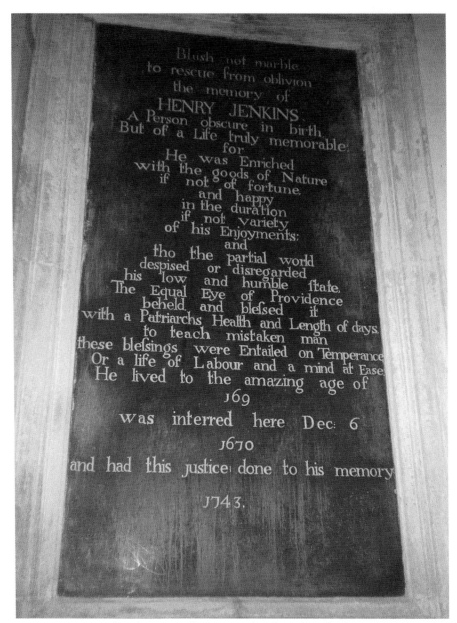

Henry Jenkins' memorial stone in the churchyard of St Mary's,
Bolton-on-Swale.

Though perhaps not a giant in stature, Henry Jenkins was most certainly a giant in terms of longevity. Unfortunately there is no definitive proof of Jenkins' amazing life span, but it is claimed that he died on 9 December 1670 at the age of one hundred and sixty-nine. His final resting place in the churchyard of St Mary's Church, Bolton-on-Swale, near Richmond, is marked by an impressive obelisk and a plaque inside the church records the virtues of this amazingly long life.

There is no verification of claims that Henry Jenkins was born at Ellerton on Swale in 1500, but it seems fairly certain that he made a living by thatching houses and other farm-related work before joining Lord Conyers' household at Hornby Castle as a butler. As claims about his advancing age gathered pace Jenkins is said to have been interviewed by a lady named Anne Saville. She questioned him about earlier events in his life, including involvement in the build-up to the Battle of Flodden Field (1513) when he recalled transporting a cartload of arrows for English forces led by the Earl of Surrey. Some 152 years later Mrs Saville's research convinced her that Henry Jenkins was in fact the age that he claimed, and reported that even in his final years he continued to enjoy a daily swim in the River Swale and walked long distances during fishing trips.

Finally, a meeting of the Tees Fishery Board on 26 October 1874 heard that a 'devil fish' had been caught in Middlesbrough Dock and when it was opened a salmon weighing 8 pounds was found in its stomach. Another member of the Board said that they were frequently found in the river and were nearly all head. [The devil fish has a broad, flat body and grows to a great size. A voracious eater, it crushes its victims.]

8 Puzzles in Stone & Turf

Some aspects of our heritage, both man-made and natural, never fail to tantalise, frustrate and fascinate. Simple stone circles such as the one that lies on Wayworth Moor, about 1½ miles west of Commondale, create endless debate about their origins and purpose. This feature is probably the best example of any of the stone circles to be found on the North York Moors and consists of sixteen upright stones measuring up to 3 feet in height. Measuring about 60 feet in diameter it has a tumulus, on the south-western edge, which may have served as an altar platform, and expert opinion seems to agree that the circle was constructed as an outdoor temple for Neolithic folk.

Many stories have inscriptions ranging from the wording on the Saxon sun-dial at Kirkdale, near Helmsley, to the classical phrases on mill buildings in remote Bransdale – but one of the strangest must be the lettering on a stone column behind the church at Nether Silton which reads:

> H T G O M H S
> T B B W O T G W W G
> T W O T E W A H H
> A T C L A B W H E Y
> A D 1765
> A W P S A Y A A

It turns out to be a rather lengthy mnemonic, which was carved on the orders of Squire Hickes in the eighteenth century and may be deciphered as:

Here the grand old manor house stood. The black beams were oak, the great walls were good; the walls of the east wing are hidden here; a thatched cottage like a barn was here erected year AD 1765; a wide porch spans a yard and alcove.

The curious inscription on a standing stone behind Nether Silton
Church.

Knaresborough's Dropping Well.

Brimham Moor is a wilderness of heather and bracken at an altitude of almost 1,000 feet above sea level. It is also a fine vantage point for superb views across Nidderdale and the Plain of York as well as home to a whole range of wildlife, but the abiding attraction is the collection of strangely shaped rocks that rise from a spreading carpet of heather and bracken. Scattered across 60 acres these huge outcrops of stone, collectively known as Brimham Rocks, have been shaped by a constant battering from the elements. Some are huge grotesque forms, some look like prehistoric monsters turned to stone and others seem to have been sculpted by giant hands. Four have been termed 'Rocking Stones', with the largest one weighing 100 tons; another is known as 'the Idol', and stands on a natural pedestal measuring only about 12 inches in width. A pair of rocks with a natural arch locked together by a keystone have been given the name 'Lovers' Leap' while others have been termed 'the Druids' Caves' and the 'Canon Rocks' (after strange rounded windows). A whole menagerie of animal-like rocks are affectionately referred to as a rabbit, tiger, tortoise, dog and rhinoceros. Another pair are known as a yoke of oxen, and completing this incredible zoo are a dancing bear and a baboon weighing an estimated 40 tons.

There are more curious stone features at Knaresborough's Dropping Well where the water can literally turn items into stone. The water, which runs over an overhanging rock before falling like a silver curtain into a huge rock cavity, contains a strong lime content that acts as a petrifying agent. A bizarre collection of items strung across the vertical face of the well usually includes hats, boots, birds, animals and assorted oddities which are slowly being turned into stone.

Puzzles can be frustrating – if not infuriating – but the simple turf maze on a country lane between Brandsby and Darlby is simplicity itself. Measuring about 26 × 22 feet, there's no chance of getting lost among the low turf-topped walls and plenty of time to take in the superb views across the Plain of York away to the south. During the medieval period there were hundreds of turf mazes around the country but by the sixteenth century most of them had fallen into disrepair. Today there are less than a dozen of these mazes in England and this one, known as the 'City of Troy', is the only example in Yorkshire. As the name implies, this particular maze is surrounded with echoes of

The 'City of Troy' maze near Brandsby.

City of Troy.

Moorsholm's stone troughs, known as the docks!

ancient Greece, and reaching the centre of the maze symbolised death before a successful route out again represented resurrection. Local folklore suggests that bad luck will come the way of anyone who picks their way round the maze more than nine times.

Names can be so misleading, can't they? The East Cleveland village of Moorsholm is the location for a tantalising structure known as Moorsholm Docks, but any unwitting visitor would look in vain for ships, wharves or quayside features. In fact, the 'docks' in question are no more than a set of roadside stone troughs for livestock passing through this pleasant rural setting to the east of the A171 Guisborough to Whitby road. Probably originating from the late nineteenth century, these sturdy stone basins have been restored in recent years and serve as an intriguing reminder of this area's agricultural past.

9 Spa Crazy

Health matters figure prominently in most people's list of personal priorities with considerations such as diet and fitness routines taking up large measures of time and expenditure. But what's new in this? Down the years fads and patent cures have preoccupied generation after generation and in the early nineteenth century this search for the elusive elixir of life caused people to go 'spa crazy'.

The fad for 'taking the waters' saw people flocking from far and wide not only to the renowned centres such as Bath or Harrogate, where more than eighty natural springs supplied pump rooms and suites of baths, but also to any number of other towns and villages.

Coastal resorts, such as Scarborough, enjoyed the additional advantages of sandy beaches and bracing seaside breezes, and the first spa buildings were opened here at the end of the seventeenth century. High tides and landslips destroyed these original premises and the impressive group of buildings that are seen today date from the late nineteenth century. Spring water at Saltburn was found to be similar to supplies found at Harrogate, and when the Italian Gardens were laid out as an additional attraction the mineral spring was re-routed to a fountain where metal drinking cups were available.

Further inland, there were spas at Malton, Hovingham and Slapewath near Guisborough, where a mineral spring was discovered during 1822. Visitors made their way to this wooded location for several years but operations never seem to have reached the same scale as at other local health resorts. Spa buildings were becoming derelict by the 1850s and the ironstone mining that began in close proximity to the mineral spring in 1864–5 ruled out a possible revival in its fortunes. North Yorkshire's most popular spa village was probably Croft on Tees, where the earliest spa was opened in 1669 when Sir William Chaytor created a horse pond close to a sulphur well

Valley Gardens, Saltburn-by-the-Sea, close to the spa.

Italian Gardens, Saltburn-by-the-Sea.

Spa Wood near Guisborough, where an ironstone mine covered the site formerly occupied by a health spa.

Croft Spa, from the bridge across the River Tees.

in order to treat two of his horses. Another spa was opened some 300 yards from Croft Bridge in 1827 when Sir William's grandson built a pump room over the spring and then added a suite of baths. By 1837 some eight hundred clients were taking regular baths in the waters from sulphur, magnesium and chalybeate springs (chalybeate is a salt rich in iron). During the early nineteenth century Croft's spa waters had achieved national popularity and fetched a high price when sold in sealed jars in London. The Spa Hotel is mentioned in 1704 as a coaching inn serving travellers on the Great North Road. A new building had taken shape by 1808 as visitors flocked to Croft in search of the health-giving waters (and further extensive restoration work was carried out in 1973). By 1841 the craze was waning and the number of people visiting the spas at Croft had declined considerably. Today the only material signs of this boom period are the remains of walkways, wells and bridges in the neighbouring woodland.

Spa buildings at Croft.

Bedale Leech House.

North Yorkshire's coastal resorts are rather hilly and local lads showed commendable business initiative at Saltburn-by-the-Sea. Realising that some visitors may have limited mobility and difficulty in reaching the spa or shoreline they followed Mark Burton's horse-drawn water cart round the township, offering to take buckets of health-giving seawater to guests' rooms at a cost of just *2d* per bucket!

On the subject of health matters, Bedale has a tiny, unique building that was used as a leech house from the late eighteenth or early nineteenth centuries into the early twentieth. Fresh water from the adjacent beck was channelled through the red-brick building in order to keep the leeches in prime condition before delivery to local doctors. At one time they were used on a wide scale to draw blood from patients with almost any ailment. By 1985 the leech house was in a derelict state, but Bedale District Heritage Trust orchestrated a restoration scheme and this curious little structure has been granted Grade II listed status by English Heritage.

10 Monsters – Separating Fact from Fiction

Mythology, folklore and church carvings provide many examples of monsters, dragons, wyverns or fiery serpents, and most areas have their own collection of monster legends. It is all too easy to dismiss these creatures as products of our ancestors' fertile imaginations and their ignorance of relevant branches of science, but even in today's world of advanced technology we are left with unexplained reports and unsubstantiated claims from the 'Yeti' of the Himalayan slopes and 'Big Foot' in North American forests to the Loch Ness monster and sightings of 'big cats' in rural parts of the north country; these mysterious stories persist.

Handale, near Loftus, was the location for a Benedictine nunnery for about 400 years between its foundation by the Percy family in 1133 until closure during 1532. Stonework from the priory has largely disappeared but in 1830 several curious discoveries were made. In addition to sixteen skeletons, a coffin was unearthed with an inscription on the lid, which was translated as 'Snake Killer'. Inside the coffin were a skeleton and a sword measuring more than 4 feet in length, and speculation links these discoveries with a local legend involving a bold youth named Scaw who rescued young maidens from the clutches of a huge snake. The prisoners were said to be held in a cave within nearby woods and Scaw had to overcome the monster's fearsome fumes before doing battle. After a desperate struggle he won the day and was rewarded by marriage to the daughter of a local noble. The area of woodland where the dramatic battle took place became known as Scaw's Wood.

There is a similar story at Sexhow, near Swainby, where a fearsome serpent was alleged to have its lair in nearby Whorl Hill. Demands for

The site of Handale Priory and location for the Handale monster legend.

The farm on the site of Handale Priory, close to Scaw Wood.

food, drink and slaves were silenced when a brave young knight tracked down the monster and came out victorious after an epic encounter.

The story surrounding the Dragon of Loschy Wood, near Stonegrave (south of Helmsley), has several other intriguing aspects. This venomous monster not only breathed fire and smoke but also had a poisoned tongue and teeth as large as the prongs of a pitchfork. Not surprisingly, many gallant knights had tried in vain to overcome the gargantuan beast until another local hero, named Peter, used guile and cunning in his planned assault. Before facing the dragon, he hired a local metalsmith to make a suit of armour covered with razor blades with the edges facing outwards. As the serpent wrapped itself around the intrepid knight the edges of the razor blades cut it in a hundred or more places. With a howl of pain and rage the ugly beast uncoiled, allowing the knight to strike out with his sword – only for the monster to roll on the ground to heal its wounds. Hour after hour the skirmish continued, for each time Peter inflicted a wound on the dragon it closed over, and it was his dog that finally won the day. After cutting off one of the monster's limbs, he whistled to the

A view towards Whorl Hill, lair of the legendary Sexhow Worm.

Former railway buildings at Sexhow, hunting ground of the monster.

dog, which promptly rushed into the combat and made off with the severed section. Leaving it close to Nunnington Church, the dog watched the struggle until the knight cut off another portion of the dragon. Again he ran in, picked up the fragment and carried it away. In this way the knight and his dog reduced the dragon limb by limb, until only the head was left, and when this was carried off to a nearby hillside the struggle was over. Sadly this tale did not have a happy ending. As the knight congratulated his dog it licked his face. On its tongue was some of the poison from the dragon's body, and instantly the knight fell dead. Soon afterwards the dog died of a broken heart.

Some of these stories add a gruesome touch by stating that the skin of the vanquished foe was afterwards displayed on the back of the local church door. Accepting that these tales have been embellished and exaggerated down the centuries, how do we account for the frequency and persistence of these unlikely sagas? Some theories point to the fact that until fairly recent times most of our upland areas were covered in woodland that provided cover for wolves, boars and even bears (in the

Nunnington Church has links with the dragon of nearby Loschy Wood.

Track between Nunnington and West Ness, territory of the local legendary dragon.

early medieval period). Others point to the possible presence of a large eel at locations close to rivers and waterways, but the most likely link is probably with Viking raiders who penetrated northern parts in the pre-Norman period. Sailing their longships into river estuaries before manhandling them into strategic locations, the subjugation of native people, demands for slaves or supplies of food and drink under the threatening presence of the dragonhead prow of their vessels probably gave rise to these monster legends.

Monsters from a much earlier age are still being uncovered along the Yorkshire coast to the north of Whitby. The headland around Kettleness has been scarred by extensive alum workings, which have left behind barren slopes of loose grey shale, and this setting has provided the largest fossils found along the Yorkshire coast. During the Lower Jurassic period huge marine reptiles, including plesiosaurs, ichthyosaurus and crocodiles swam in the shallow waters of these parts, and when they died their remains rested in the soft shale of the

Hummersea, near Loftus, close to coastal alum workings where fossils of huge prehistoric reptiles have been recovered.

seabed. Eventually the seas retreated and today's land mass emerged, but the collection of fossilised bones remained undisturbed for over 180 million years. Extraction of alum shale began in the early seventeenth century and as headlands were excavated thousands of different fossils were exposed. Victorian geologists and historians appreciated the value of these impressive remains and many specimens were carefully excavated and put on permanent display. The largest reptile fossil to be discovered in this area was a plesiosaur, *Rhomaleosaurus cramptoni*, which was excavated in 1848 and is now housed in the National Museum of Ireland. There is also a cast at the Natural History Museum, London, and examples are on display in local museums such as the Yorkshire Museum, York, and Pannett Park Museum, Whitby. Alum mining operations ended in the mid-nineteenth century but erosion of the coastline has continued to reveal more huge fossils, including a complete ichthyosaur that was revealed in 1999.

11 Disappearing Racecourses & Strange Sporting Occasions

N orth Yorkshire has a long-standing connection with horses and the sport of kings, and training stables as well as race meetings are still found at several locations. While these days large crowds are still drawn to venues such as York, Redcar, Thirsk, Northallerton and Ripon, reminders of dramatic sporting occasions at Richmond, Thornaby, Picton, Malton and Hambleton are few and far between.

Thornaby's course has disappeared in recent years under a retail park and races at Langton Wold near Malton ended as long ago as 1862. Race meetings were well established on the Wold by 1692 and it was here that John Scott, 'The Wizard of the North', trained forty-one Classic winners, a record that stands today. When racing ended some one hundred and forty years ago the grandstand was turned into a farmhouse and much of the course was ploughed up. Training continues on the eastern part of the old course and strings of racehorses from stables in nearby Malton and Norton pass through the pretty village of Langton on most days of the year. About a mile to the north-west of Richmond market place is the grandstand of the town's former racecourse. Dating from 1775, it has five bays across the frontage and a lower arcade of Tuscan columns with an iron balcony running all round. The starter's stand also survives and there are long-term plans to restore the course to its earlier glory.

The most unlikely location for a racecourse was at Hambleton on level ground at the top of Sutton Bank, where underlying peat

Richmond racecourse: the small structure at the starting gate.

Dialstone Farm, close to Sutton Bank and the former Hambleton racecourse.

Dialstone Farm. A stone from the racecourse weighing machine was built into a nearby drystone wall.

supports a springy surface in even the driest of conditions. According to entries in Thomas Chaytor's diaries racing was well established at Hambleton by 1612 and by 1714 there was a race for the Queen's Gold Cup, with a value of 100 guineas. In 1740 an Act of Parliament stated that races where prize money amounted to less than £50 could only be held at Newmarket, York and Hambleton. This acknowledgement of Hambleton's merits as a course was made in spite of the difficulty in reaching the remote setting, but Racing Calendar records show that the 1740 Act had made little difference, as horseracing continued at eleven other Yorkshire venues. Hambleton's importance as a northern venue for a Royal Cup continued until 1776 when it was ruled that racing for the Royal Plate should alternate between Richmond and York. This arrangement hastened the end of

Hambleton as a major racecourse, and the decline was accelerated by the development of social events based at Assembly Rooms in both York and Richmond, and the construction of grandstands at these courses for spectators. Hambleton had little to offer in terms of facilities for spectators or horses and although it continued in use as a training area the course's racing days were soon over. A reminder from these times is lodged in a stone wall at Dialstone Farm. It takes the form of a circular stone which was the base for a dial or weighing machine for weighing in jockeys.

Over the last century or so North Yorkshire has seen several strange sporting spectacles. Horses featured strongly in the meet of the Cleveland hounds at Coatham, near Redcar, in the closing days of December 1895, but they were accompanied for several miles by five well-known Redcar tradesmen mounted on bicycles. The *Daily Gazette* for 28 December 1895 reported that 'in spite of hedges, ditches and ploughed fields they kept up with the horsemen for several miles from Coatham to Lackenby Ironworks. Travelling over grass fields gave them no trouble; they negotiated the unploughed cornfields easily and even managed to ride over ploughed fields when furrows ran the way they desired to journey. At hedges and ditches they had of necessity to dismount and the "bikes" were handed over from one side to the other, so that very little time was lost and the riders were never far behind the hounds. . . . Much amusement was caused by the event, though eventually the bicycle riders had to fall behind.'

Sporting excitement came from the skies in early October 1906 when an American balloonist landed near Whitby. A story in the *Daily Gazette* of 2 October 1906 reported that sixteen balloons had left Paris on Sunday 30 September in a race for the Gordon Bennett Cup. 'The object of the race was twofold – to stay in the air as long as possible and cover as great a distance as possible. . . . The best so far was Lieutenant Lahn in the American balloon, the United States, who had succeeded in covering 440 miles after a journey lasting 24 hours.' He landed at Fylingdales near Whitby.

Cricketers are used to playing in unpleasant weather but the *Daily Gazette* for Monday 6 January 1879 reported on a highly unusual cricket match: 'On Saturday afternoon last, through the long continuance of frost, cricket clubs of the district are able to indulge in their favourite pastime on a sheet of ice near the boathouse belonging to Mr R.N. Dodds of South Stockton (Thornaby). Sides were chosen by Mr W. Smith and Mr Thomas Dickenson and wickets were pitched shortly after 10 o'clock in front of hundreds of spectators. The teams had one innings each and there were a few falls, collisions and other amusing incidents peculiar to the exercise of skating. Mr Smith's side scored 126 and Mr Dickenson's 143.' Plans were made for an 'improved' game and this took place on Saturday 11 January when the Lyall brothers organised the event on an ice-bound field.

Middlesbrough has been a hotbed of soccer for many years but it's doubtful if any of the team's footballers expect to appear on the stage! A show at the town's Empire Theatre in December 1956 was billed as 'Sensations of 1956 . . . including personal appearances at every performance of Middlesbrough's most popular footballers Brian Clough, the League's top scoring centre forward, v Lindy Delapena – one of the most brilliant forwards in the league – featuring the Television Sensation Football Tennis actually played at every performance for the Challenge Cup.'

12 Superstitions & Unusual Ceremonies

In today's world of advanced technology and high speed living it's reassuring that there is still time and space for long-standing superstitions and unusual ceremonies.

The Saltersgate Inn stands by the side of the A169 close to the Hole of Horcum on the North York Moors. Several tracks link up at the inn, and in earlier days lines of packhorses carried salt and fish inland from the coast around Whitby. The inn dates from 1648 and is believed to have been at the heart of smuggling activities with a tiny window manned by a lookout. On occasion violence broke out between smugglers and excise officers and during one altercation a man received fatal injuries; he was supposedly buried under the hearth of the peat fire at the inn. One story claims that the fire has been burning ever since to prevent his ghost from escaping. Another version of the story is that an old hermit, who lived in the remote Hole of Horcum during the eighteenth century, chided the landlord that if the peat fire went out then the building would be destroyed. Whatever the origins of the tale, the fire is said to have burned ever since. Similar slow burning fires are said to have smouldered year after year at the Chequers Inn near Osmotherley and Huckaback Farm, close to Castleton.

Busby Stoop Inn at Sandhutton near Thirsk was the setting for a sequence of extremely unpleasant events in the early eighteenth century. Tom Busby attacked his father-in-law Daniel Auty with a hammer and beat him to death after an argument over money. In the eighteenth century it was the custom to hang a convicted man on the spot where he committed the crime and then gibbet the corpse beside the public highway. Busby's body was left to rot on gallows close to the crossroads near the inn, and not only is his ghost said to haunt the premises but

Chequers Inn on the drovers' road near Osmotherley.

he is also said to have placed a curse on his chair inside the hostelry. Anyone sitting in the simple wooden seat would be cursed by the ghost to die within weeks. Down the years the sombre forecast has come true – with a number of sudden and unexpected deaths after a victim has sat in the chair. Now the chair has been moved from the inn to Thirsk Museum, where it is tied high up on the wall for safety's sake!

One of North Yorkshire's oldest customs takes place in Ripon at 9 o'clock every evening when an official horn blower, called the Wakeman, sounds a horn at the mayor's house and the market cross. In 1986 the city of Ripon celebrated the 1,100th anniversary of receiving its charter in the form of a horn from King Alfred the Great. A similar ceremony takes place some 30 miles away at Bainbridge during the dark days of winter. Between 28 September and Shrove Tuesday three blasts on the horn are sounded every evening towards each point of the compass. The purpose was to serve as a signal for

Huckaback Farm, Castleton, and another long-burning fire.

Busby Stoop Inn, near Thirsk.

Ripon market place obelisk and the setting for the hornblowing ceremony.

Bainbridge village green, setting for another hornblowing ceremony.

gathering sheep from neighbouring slopes and to help the shepherd find his way home in the darkness. Traditional horn blowers at Bainbridge are drawn from the Metcalfe family of Nappa Hall, and the horn is kept at the Rose and Crown Inn.

Another ancient ceremony takes place each year in the upper harbour at Whitby. On the day before Ascension Day bundles of stakes and thin branches are carried to the harbour side for a 9 am start to proceedings. A penny hedge is erected at the water's edge and it has to be strong enough to survive three tides. The custom is said to have originated as an act of penance imposed on three hunters by the abbot of Whitby in 1159. The wrongdoers were chasing a boar, which took refuge in a hermit's cave, and during the ensuing mêlée the hermit suffered fatal injuries. Another explanation claims that the penny hedge derives from an early fish trap.

Horngarth in the upper harbour at Whitby.

Remains of the penny hedge in June 1999.

Goathland village green.

At noon on Shrove Tuesday the pancake bell is rung in Scarborough's museum to announce to the local population that pancake making can get under way. Traditionally there are skipping contests on the foreshore with the emphasis on participation by everyone present.

Traditional sword dances have survived in various parts of the North Country including the Eskdale area of North Yorkshire. Using swords measuring 30 to 40 inches in length and made of steel or wood, the dances are performed by teams of six or eight men. The origins of these ceremonies are clouded in uncertainty but it is likely that they are the only surviving component of annual folk plays. Sword dancers have traditionally performed at Goathland on Plough Monday in January. One of their characters is named Isaac, or t'Awd Man, and the group is known as the Plough Stots. Reports suggest

Croft Bridge, where the ceremony involving the Conyers falchion takes place.

that they used to plough a furrow in the lawns of people who would not pay them for their performance.

Even more dramatic action takes place at West Witton, Wensleydale, on the Saturday closest to St Bartholomew's Day (24 August). The Bartle, a large straw effigy, is carried through the village after nightfall before it is burnt on a bonfire. As the procession makes its way through the village an old rhyme is recited by local folk. The Bartle is said to have been an eighteenth-century cattle thief who was pursued over nearby hillsides before being captured and put to death.

Croft Bridge is the setting for an interesting and unusual ceremony involving the Prince Bishops of Durham. The last Prince Bishop was Van Mildert and he took part in the ceremony on the centre of this fine seven-arched bridge during 1826. This same ceremony took place in 1860 when Henry Montague Villiers was welcomed as Bishop of Durham. He travelled to the diocese by rail, and the train stopped in the middle of the nearby railway bridge over the Tees so that he could

The river in flood at Croft Bridge.

be presented with the falchion by a representative of the Lord of Sockburn. Proceedings involved presentation of the Conyers falchion to the Bishop by the Lords of the Manor of Sockburn. The Conyers falchion is a broadsword, which was alleged to have been used to slay the legendary Sockburn Worm. (It was presented to the Dean and Chapter of Durham in 1947 – a gift from the last Lord of the Manor of Sockburn – and is now on display in Durham Cathedral.) The sword was returned to the Lord of Sockburn along with hopes for good health and a long stay at the Manor. The ceremony was revived on 20 September 1984 when Dr David Jenkins was welcomed into his diocese by the Mayor of Darlington.

Until about a century ago it was widely believed in northern England that on St Mark's Eve (24 April) the spirits of people who would die during the next twelve months haunted local churchyards between 11 pm and 1 am. Needless to say, a number of old men used to gather in church porches to keep a morbid watch!

13 The Devil Himself

It is hard to imagine in the twenty-first century how much of our ancestors' lives were dominated by a deep belief in supernatural matters. The Kingdom of Darkness, with its devils and evil spirits, was as real and personal as the Kingdom of Heaven. The idea of supernatural spirits was universal, and ordinary folk believed in demons, imps and hobgoblins as well as legendary monsters and intimidating giants. The prime mover in these realms of superstition and trepidation was the Prince of Darkness himself, ably supported by legions of handmaidens . . . witches.

Three centuries ago people's everyday lives were dominated by an all-embracing code of religious beliefs that featured references to heaven and angels ranged against the forces of evil marshalled by large numbers of witches under their mentor in chief . . . the Devil. In today's world of high technology and virtual reality it is easy to discount and dismiss such views, but the reality of this world of darkness to our forebears can be found in the many references to the Prince of Darkness.

Many areas have a 'Devil's Bridge', and more often than not there are associated tales of Old Nick lurking beneath the bridge's arch ready to waylay unsuspecting travellers along the highway. Newham Bridge crosses Marton West Beck on the south-east side of Acklam, and is said to mark the line of an early route that crossed the Tees in the Newport area and then ran in a southerly direction towards the North Yorkshire coast. With housing closing in from the west and a cycleway crossing the single span stone structure there is little to remind us of the folk tales linked with this Devil's Bridge.

There is a variation on the usual theme involving a shoemaker named Ralph Calvert who made the regular journey from his home at Thorpe to Fountains Abbey. After sharing his eel pie and wine with a

Devil's Bridge, Acklam.

fellow traveller – the Devil – Calvert requested that his newfound friend should build a bridge over the River Dibble. To everyone's astonishment, so the story runs, the fine stone bridge was completed in just three days.

A number of landscape features are linked with the Devil. The almost circular natural hollow called the Hole of Horcum is known locally as the Devil's Punchbowl, while the sharp bend in the A169 at the bottom of Saltersgate Bank is known as the Devil's Elbow.

Butter Tubs Pass links Muker in Swaledale with Hawes in Wensleydale and rises to an altitude of 1,726 feet at its highest point. Near the summit is a series of strange vertical shafts in the limestone landscape with a depth of between 50 and 100 feet. Geologists verify that they are entirely natural but in earlier days they were known as 'the Devil's Footsteps'.

The Devil's Arrows, near Boroughbridge.

A narrow passage under cliff faces along the Hambleton Hills is known as 'the Devil's Parlour' because of the dangers facing those who try to explore this claustrophobic cavern.

Fossils were also associated with the Prince of Darkness. Fossil belemnites were said to be an actual thunderbolt fired by the Devil and our gullible ancestors felt that this belief was reinforced when they were washed to the surface of soft clay soils during heavy rainstorms. Alternatively they were known as 'Devil's Fingers'. The fossil oyster gryphaea was known as the Devil's toenail, and although it was supposed to ward off rheumatism and arthritis there is no scientific basis for this long-held belief.

One of Yorkshire's best-known monuments has the collective name of 'the Devil's Arrows'. Three natural stones ranging in height from 16 to 22 feet stand close to the A1 road on the south-west side of

The north door,
traditionally known as the
Devil's Door, at Lythe
Church near Sandsend.

Boroughbridge. A fourth stone was broken up to construct a bridge over the little River Tutt more than three hundred years ago. As a result of weathering they now have a fluted shape at the top and it has been established that these amazing columns of millstone grit were quarried some 6½ miles away to the south-west at Knaresborough. Lines of stones are far less common than stone circles (which were used for religious purposes) and archaeologists are unclear about their purpose, although it seems likely that they date from the Bronze Age period.

The north door of Anglican churches has become known as 'the Devil's door' through which the Prince of Darkness is said to have fled when a child was brought into the building for baptism. Doorways on the north side are said to have led to the cold, cheerless and sunless region of darkness and night while the proper entrance to the church, on the south, was lit by sunlight that shone through into the building. There are fine examples of north doorways in the splendid churches at Thirsk and South Kilvington.

According to a report in 1857 the churchyard at Kirkby Malham was the setting for a midnight banquet prepared by the Devil on an unspecified date. The vicar, the Revd Martin Knowles, and a young boy named Kitchen were invited to the feast which was set out on a gravestone, but the whole event came to an abrupt halt, so the story goes, when the parson requested salt. At this point, it is said, the Devil and all the food disappeared!

North country superstitions even linked the world of nature with the Devil. The collective name 'Devil's Flowers' was given to a whole range of flowers which had an unpleasant smell or were poisonous. These included deadly nightshade, sun spurge, yarrow, stitchwort, wild garlic, ragwort and hemlock.

Another old North Country saying ruled that it was unlucky to eat blackberries during October. This belief arises from Michaelmas Day (29 September) being cited as the time when Satan was thrown out of Heaven. It is said that he fell into a thorny bramble bush and promptly cursed it. Since then, it is said, he has spoiled each bramble harvest on Michaelmas Day by scorching, spitting or stamping on them.

WITCHCRAFT

Belief in witchcraft persisted throughout the medieval period and during the late sixteenth and early seventeenth centuries, and there was widespread persecution of these unfortunate women. The popular idea of a witch in towns and country villages was an ugly old hag twisted with age who usually kept company with mice or toads or other 'familiar spirits' secretly given to her by the Devil. Every witch was believed to have a 'devil mark' somewhere on his or her body, and although the last execution for witchcraft took place in 1684, at Exeter, court cases continued into recent times with the prosecution of a retired army veteran in 1947. He had assaulted a woman after claiming she had bewitched him with a bunch of flowers!

Many North Yorkshire villages had a resident witch. These included Peggy Flounders of Marske, Peg Humphrey, based at East Moors near Helmsley, Jane Grear from Guisborough and Nan Hardwicke who lived near Danby. Betty Strother came from the Castleton area and was said to be a sorceress although she only practised white magic. Many local folk called on Betty to buy patent cures and good luck charms for themselves and also for their livestock. She is said to have possessed great healing powers, which she inherited from her mother, and her regalia included a crystal ball, magic looking glass, magic cubes and witch's garter. Stories about her magical powers spread far and wide and on one occasion she is said to have been called on to purify a butter churn that had been cursed by the Devil. Betty prepared a powder, which was poured into the churn, and before long, so the story runs, a serpent emerged from the vessel. It took on the form of the Devil and rapidly disappeared from view.

It was widely believed that a witch could turn herself into an animal such as a cat, frog, hedgehog or, most commonly, a hare. Stories of witch hares persisted until recent times and in the majority of these tales a hare is chased towards the house of a suspected witch where the animal takes refuge. When the hunters enter the building they find a witch, in human form, exhausted and terrified. In some incidents the hare has been nipped by a pursuing hound and the witch is discovered to have a similar wound. Peg Humphrey of East Moors featured in several of these reports in the late 1830s.

Although witches provided positive benefits, including potions and powders to help with matters of the heart, many people went in fear of their magical powers and took steps to keep them at bay. Hazel twigs woven into a cross and worn round the neck, horse-shoes nailed to stable doorways, corn dollies in the shape of birds to serve as a distraction and good luck charms were all used in attempts to avoid witches' spells. Many householders also built a witch post into their homes. Intended to prevent evil spirits from entering, the post was usually fixed just inside a doorway and had a St Andrew's cross carved at the top with a horizontal band (for each member of the family) at a lower point. Examples of a witch post may still be seen in cruck cottages at the Ryedale Folk Museum, Hutton-le-Hole, and at Pannett Park Museum, Whitby.

In some places, such as Esk Hall at Sleights, the witch's curse still holds strong. A wide straight drive runs down a sloping avenue of trees to the magnificent frontage of the old hall, but both ends of the driveway are fenced off and grass has grown over the drive. Legend suggests that when the drive was first opened the owner of the hall

Ryedale Folk Museum, Hutton-le-Hole, with displays from rural areas of North Yorkshire including cruck cottages and witchcraft.

was killed as he rode between the trees. Following this sad incident a witch cursed the driveway and warned that if the gates were opened a member of the family or a visitor would die within the year. The curse has claimed three victims, one of them when the owner of the hall spotted his daughter standing on the drive with the butler. He rushed through the gates to shoot the butler but tragically shot his daughter instead. New owners in 1977 decided that they were not going to reopen the driveway and continued to use the narrow side route instead.

Criminals used a ghoulish charm that they believed carried hypnotic powers. The hand of a gibbeted criminal was squeezed to drain any blood that remained in the veins and then pickled with spices and saltpetre. A candle was made up of pitch wick, the fat of a

Pannett Park Museum, Whitby, which houses a collection of North
Yorkshire materials including a witch post and a Hand of Glory.

hanged man, 'virgin wax' and mustard oil before being fixed between
the fingers. The 'Hand of Glory' as it was known was then used in
burglaries, when it was supposed to leave victims unable to move.
Reports indicate that this strange accessory was used in an attempted
burglary at the Old Spital Inn on Bowes Moor during autumn 1797,
and an example of the 'Hand of Glory' in all its sinister splendour may
still be seen at Whitby's Pannett Park Museum.

Superstition and tradition was attached to most phases of life. At
birth a child had to go up before they came down so if they were
delivered on the top storey of a house one of the women would stand
on a table, chair or chest of drawers with the babe in her arms. The
child's nails had to remain uncut during their first year of life and
after this, they were not to be cut on Friday or Saturday, as this would
bring bad luck. A bible had to be kept under the baby's pillow until the
christening in order to keep evil spirits at bay.

It was also unlucky to marry on a Friday, as it was to wear either blue or green. After the wedding service bride and groom had to leap over a form when leaving the church porch and a shotgun (filled with feathers) was fired over the departing couple's heads in order to scare away evil spirits. If they stepped in dirt it was unlucky to wipe it off their shoes, and once they reached the marital home there was another strange tradition: the bride was offered cake and after eating a small portion she threw the remainder over her head to ensure that they would have plenty in future. Her husband then threw the plate over his shoulder; if it broke, the couple were assured of future happiness.

All sorts of superstitions were linked with everyday incidents. A stumble on the stairs meant that you would be married within the year . . . if a hair thrown on the fire burns for a long time it means long life . . . an itchy nose means you're going to be angry or kissed by a fool . . . an itchy foot indicates that you will soon step on strange ground and, among the many means of forecasting future climatic conditions, a star close to the moon indicates a bout of impending bad weather.

Completing this world of witchcraft, spells, charms and superstitions was a whole legion of 'wee folk' in the guise of grims, hobs, bogles and bargests. Almost every village, it seems, had its own resident hob or similar tiny creature who exercised a considerable influence on everyday life. More often than not, they helped with tasks around the farm or home, like the hob at Hob Hill, Upleatham, who is said to have threshed corn or turned hay until he was spotted by a member of the Oughtred family. As an act of goodwill the family made him a new coat but this only served to infuriate the temperamental hob who responded by smashing crockery and breaking machinery. It took a special ceremony at dead of night to rid the household of this outraged little fellow. A similar story is told at Hart Hall, Glaisdale, where a hob helped with farming tasks until he was spotted by a young member of the household. Taking pity on him, the family made a coarse shirt to provide warmth during the winter months, but this only served to upset the hob who promptly left Hart Hall for ever.

14 Out of Print – A Miscellany

Local newspapers are an invaluable source of information, but some of the reported incidents are almost beyond belief! A report in the *North Eastern Daily Gazette* on 21 April 1874 gave details of a strike by members of a church choir in the Eston area:

> Complaints have been made as to particular members of the choir . . . indulging in certain amusements in church which were hardly the proper thing . . . such as reading novels, drinking whisky, chewing tobacco etc. Some members of the church choir considered that they were unjustly accused in participating in the acts of others and the result is that the whole choir have struck and the congregation are, for the time being, deprived of the luxury of a musical service.

In March 1907 the curate of New Marske called for abstinence from a whole range of foods and activities, including 'flesh meat or cigars and cigarettes, or more than one glass of beer. . . . Or all unnecessary amusement or dancing or frolicking or lovemaking.' However, one local observer noted, 'I see no diminution in the couples walking out. Perhaps this may cause pain to the Reverend gentleman, but let us hope that an epidemic of weddings will make up for any disappointment he may experience in their direction.'

A strange bottle was handed to staff at Whitby Museum in March 1936. Investigation revealed that one of the uses to which the bottle was put was to chase evil spirits from cows or other animals said to have been 'witched'. The bottle was rubbed on the animal's head, along its back, across its loins and then down along its tail chasing the 'devil' off the tail end.

It is also said that when a light was shone through the bottle, all sorts of fearful and wonderful events to come were shadowed on the wall. There was probably some ritual connected with the use of the bottle.

There was a very different vision in a bottle of tap water at Yarm in March 1939, when a local resident handed the offending glassware to the Parish Council. Captain Tate identified the bottle's contents as a freshwater shrimp. He reported that it happened quite often when he first went to live at Yarm in 1921, but could not understand how it got through the modern filter plant. The bottle, complete with shrimp, was sent to the Sanitary Inspector of Stokesley Rural District Council for further investigation.

During the years of the Second World War Teesside and North Yorkshire suffered a number of air raids on industrial targets. One Middlesbrough woman was unfortunate enough to be injured by a relic from hostilities that took place well over twenty years earlier. A report on 2 November 1942 explained that a lady from Croft Street had been admitted to the North Riding Infirmary during the previous evening with a fractured leg. Her injuries were caused by a shell from the First World War, which had stood on her mantelpiece as an ornament for twenty-four years. When her fire grate broke she took it down and used it as a support for the front. Neighbours heard a sizzling noise and then an explosion as the fireplace was blown out, sending shrapnel flying into the walls. One neighbour had been present when the lady polished the shell and put it into the grate, but left before the dramatic outcome.

Index of Place Names

Owing to boundary changes some of these towns are no longer considered to be in Yorkshire, but they formed part of the old North Riding.